The History
of the
Patchwork Quilt

The History
of the
Patchwork Quilt

Origins, Traditions and Symbols of a textile art

Schnuppe von Gwinner

1469 Morstein Road, West Chester, Pennsylvania 19380

Translated from German by Dr. Edward Force

This work was originally published in German as *Die Geschichte des Patchworkquilts* by Keyser Book Publishing Ltd., Munich, 1987.

English edition copyright © 1988 by Schiffer Publishing Ltd.
Library of Congress Catalog Number: 88-61477.

Printed in the United States of America.
ISBN: 0-88740-136-8
Published by Schiffer Publishing Ltd.
1469 Morstein Road, West Chester, Pennsylvania 19380

This book may be purchased from the publisher.
Please include $2.00 postage.
Try your bookstore first.

Contents

Foreword

To an increasing degree, the patchwork quilt is enjoying great popularity, even in Europe. It is a medium of creative artistry as well as a textile antiquity, an anthropological collectable as well as a product of modern design. The many exhibitions in the museums of large German and European cities in recent years are a clear indication. A selection of old North American quilts from the American Folk Art Museum in New York was shown in Munich and Hamburg in 1982 and 1983, and the significant Verena Klüser collection of antique quilts was displayed in Krefeld in 1983 and Karlsruhe in 1985. Anthropological patchwork could be seen, for example, within the parameters of the display of Osmanli art in Frankfurt and Essen in 1985, as well as in the Afghanistan exhibition at the Munich Anthropological Museum early in 1986. There was a show of modern American patchwork designs in Mulhouse in 1985, while the Quilt Biennial in the Heidelberg Textile Museum presents the work of German-speaking textile artists regularly since 1984.

So there is sufficient cause to examine the origins, traditions and symbolism of the patchwork quilt, especially as the existing German-language literature has thus far concentrated on pure technique and left little space for history.

The intent of this book is, first of all, to provide the reader with a consolidated survey of the many-faceted background of this textile art. In this respect, the literature cited in the bibliography is of much importance, for at bottom the theme of each chapter would be substantial enough to be treated as the theme of a separate book. A glossary, on the other hand, was deliberately omitted, since the technical and substantive concepts relevant to patchwork and quilts had to be explained in the text. A general explanation of individual technical terms concerning textile terminology, as they are not mentioned in the footnotes, have been too vast.

No sufficiently thorough scientific examination of European and anthropological patchwork textiles has yet been undertaken. It might be hoped that, inspired by my study and based on the listed literature on the subject, a few gaps could yet be filled in. In the English-language literature on the subject, this lack has meanwhile been recognized too, as indicated by several recent publications, particularly about Asiatic traditions.

The dominance of the North American patchwork quilt, with its broad cultural influence, is obvious. The books published on the subject, with their wealth of knowledge and thoroughness, give impressive evidence of that.

A focal point of my work lay, above all, in including, to as great a degree as possible, material available to me in Germany and Switzerland, or at least in Europe. These efforts were meant to show how important the subject is to us, even though the very term "patchwork" makes our thoughts spring over the Atlantic, no matter how unwillingly. A look into the possessions of almost all the large European museums is very worthwhile for the seeker. But the willingness of private collectors to cooperate by displaying their treasures and sharing their knowledge was truly overwhelming. I hereby thank them with all my heart.

Here in Germany one who knows, loves and collects patchwork quilts can still do pioneering work in the field. If my first steps can offer a foundation and an inspiration for others to go farther, then my work has fulfilled its intention.

Schnuppe von Gwinner

Introduction

We unintentionally link the concept of the patchwork quilt with the romance of the North American pioneers and the colorful bedclothes that can be seen in old Wild West movies. It is synonymous with North American folk art, in which a way was found to turn material necessity into many new forms of decoration so typical of that art.

Patchwork quilts are by definition articles that are sewn together out of pieces of fabric and then quilted. In this book the concept of patchwork, "the work of patching", will be understood to include applique, or sewing one piece on top of another, as well as sewing one piece next to another.

One finds patchwork in almost all the world's cultures. Bedouin women join fabrics that they weave into tent strips, while in Dahomey in West Africa, umbrellas and ceremonial clothes for festive occasions are sewn by the applique technique. Patchwork quilts belong among the trousseau of an Indian bride and the battle dress of Northwest African warriors.

Above and beyond all utility, they serve a people's need for decoration and give free rein to their creative talents. The patterns, whether geometric or figured, take on the power of symbols, as is common to all arts. It is not by chance that patchwork textiles have been used as ceremonial cloths and festival hangings. In both real and symbolic terms, they separate the everyday from the festivity the ordinary from the extraordinary that attains its deeper significance only in festival rites.

Though the patchwork tradition is at home in almost every culture, the American pioneer women of the 19th Century have won the fame of achieving its richest development. The origin of this textile art form that is so beloved today could not have been a single stroke of genius; rather the roots of this tradition are widely branched. They are found in the greatest variety of cultural, social and industrial development, and will be described for the first time in this book.

The basis of my study is provided by the richness of English-language literature that has been published in the last fifty years. But we cannot simply repeat the American point of view. Our European viewpoint is different from the American, and we as Europeans are more or less outsiders. In North America patchwork quilts are a familiar part of cultural history; they are still made and used today. The historical and cultural background must first be explained to the European, so that he can recognize how his own cultural traditions also live on in the patchwork quilt.

Old catalogs and magazines have also proved to be rich sources of patchwork research material, as well as 18th and 19th-Century novels and historical studies of textile technology.

But all theoretical knowledge comes alive and becomes useful only through seeing patchwork quilts of all ages and origins. The experience to be gained by looking at as many quilts as possible cannot be replaced by any book, but can at best be strengthened thereby. So my study shall be a guide to see for yourself. In reference to any one particular quilt, general information such as is given in this book is of necessity incomplete. But out of the total mass of collected facts, along with illustrations from which patterns and technical details can be read, one can make the information that applies to this particular piece into a nearly complete picture.

Since the mid-Sixties we claim to have recognized the artistic value of traditional patchwork quilts, after having hauled them out of furniture vans where they had given good service as wadded packing material. In their patterns and color combinations were seen the forerunners of modern art motifs, and this discovery was fascinating.

Since then, patchwork fans have been divided into two camps. One group is interested only in the design and the artistic expression. They hardly understand the others, who are concerned with the origin of quiltmaking in a traditional sense. The latter, and there are many of them, at least in America, have never stopped quilting. They follow old family traditions in this activity and are interested most of all in the old values that the quilts incorporate, as Jonathan Holstein comments in his foreword to "The Artist's Quilts: La Jolla Museum of Contemporary Art", by Judy Strauss.

The same author, in his 1973 book, "The Pieced Quilt—an American Design Tradition", devoted an entire chapter to a comparison between quilt patterns and modern art. The parallels, and thereby the anticipation of the folk art, are presented convincingly, even if Holstein does not take the final step of raising the quilt to the status of a work of art.

In other sources, for example Charles Dickens' novels, "Oliver Twist" and "David Copperfield", patchwork is used as a synonym for poor, ragged and dirty. For many people, even today, the association with poverty is always present when they hear the term "patchwork".

In crass contrast to all that is the approach of modern quilt makers who, since the Seventies, and particularly in America, have developed new creative ideas out of traditional textile techniques. It is only fair that their artistic interpretations, as modern quilt designs, should set standards that are new and different from all that has gone before.

Perhaps this book can help the patchwork quilt attain a status appropriate to it, between the demands of high art and the contempt of mere patching.

Quilting

We cannot tell whether patchwork or quilting is the older technique. According to American terminology, quilting will be discussed here first.

The real origins of layering and quilting techniques must lie thousands of years ago, presumably in the Orient. They came into use to strengthen textiles that had become fragile as well as to produce layered covers and clothing for protection against cold, pressure and impact. Such utilitarian textiles were especially prone to wear and tear, which explains clearly why only a few antique products of this technique have survived. In addition to its purely practical qualities, quilting also has a high decorative value, even if this developed only secondarily out of the fact that diagonal, circular, spiral or waved seams gave the fabrics greater stability than those running parallel to their weaving directions.

In quilting, the three layers of cloth, of which the central one is usually a padding of wool, cotton or other material, are held together by continual seams. A highlighting of the resulting relief character is attained by stuffing individual parts of the motif with padding or cord and sewing around them. This method is known as Italian quilting or Trapunto, since it can be traced back to the 14th Century in Sicily.

Some 800 years ago the quilting technique was brought back to Europe from the Near East by the Crusaders. In their heavy armor made of forged iron, they had fought against the Saracens in their light quilted shirts and chain mail, and had been beaten by them. So it seems to be only logical that the idea of quilted armor shirts would prevail in Europe. They were made of quilted linen stuffed with a variety of padding (#1, #2). After the introduction of firearms, there was no further need of them, but the quilting technique in general became accepted for the production of various utilitarian textiles (#4).[1]

A few quilts have survived from most European lands, thinner, two-layered linen or cotton bedclothes in Italy and France, velvet and brocade covers in the Netherlands and Germany. One must assume from them that more or less artistically quilted bedclothes of all

1 Hans Memling, Shrine of St. Ursula, side panel: the martyrdom of St. Ursula, 1498, Museum of St. John's Hospice, Bruges, Belgium. The soldier in the left foreground wears a quilted armor shirt.

2 Jörg Kölderer, Seefeld miracle panel, 1500, in the Catholic pastoral church in Seefeld, West Germany. The Miracle of Seefeld, from the year 1384, is portrayed: the knight Oswald Milser, dressed in a striped and quilted coat, requests and is given the great priests' host at communion. Afterward, according to the legend, he sank into the earth, and the host, which was still in existence at the time of World War I, took on a blood-red color.

3 Sicilian wall hanging with portrayal of the Tristan legend, circa 1395, quilting and trapunto technique, 310 x Caption for illustration 4, p. 15, via, London. 270. Victoria & Albert Museum, London.

possible fabrics must have belonged to the usual inventory, at least in well-to-do households. The quilting technique was also applied with special preference to the production of jackets and cloaks. Among the oldest known and preserved works are three Sicilian quilts of the late 14th Century (#3). They show, in several quilted panels, the legend of Tristan on a heavy two-layered linen background.[2] Seeing the perfection of this work confirms one's suspicion that quilting really must have been a widespread technique. But since it always involved textiles that wore out through daily use, only a few examples have survived until today.

4 Quilted linen blanket from Germany, 16th Century. Victoria and Albert Museum, London.

Through the discovery of America and India, and the trade that blossomed as a result, Europe earned great riches which showed particularly in the opulent life at the royal courts. The court ladies, for example, were so adorned with jewels that the ordinary silk fabrics would have torn under the weight if they had not been quilted, often with golden thread.[3]

By the Eighteenth Century, the general prosperity had grown to the extent that a comparatively large part of the population could afford better dwellings and clothing. World trade brought new textiles and yarns to Europe and inspired ideas for new forms and fashions. Quilting, especially in its highly developed form of trapunto, enhanced with costly embroidery, found more and more devotees. In general, they concentrated on producing beautiful bed coverings of linen, cotton and silk (#6).[4]

But clothing styles also made use, in a growing variety of ways, of the possibilities that quilting techniques offered (#5, 7). Many examples have survived to this day, including all imaginable types of quilted capes, jackets, petticoats and children's clothes. Quilted petticoats of silk taffeta or satin were very much in fashion, reaching their high point in the last quarter of the Eighteenth Century.[5] Quilted underclothes and work clothes have not been rare, even in our own century.[6]

Quilts themselves, with cord inlays and stuffed floral motifs, were already a widespread folk art with a tradition in southern France in the Seventeenth Century. These bedclothes were technically very advanced, as were the under- and outer skirts known as "Cotilloc", usually made of quilted white silk or linen. Cotton fabrics imported from India were worked relatively early, as were Indian and later French printed textiles (Indiennes). On high religious holidays, especially on Corpus Christi, the white bedquilts were hung out of the windows to honor the procession to church.

Since the Seventeenth Century, the southern French quilts were imported via Marseilles to England, where there was no such highly developed quilt tradition at that time. They were generally referred to as Marseilles quilts, regardless of whether they were actually quilts or hand-quilted silk yard goods out of which petticoats, linings, jackets and vests were made.

England's foreign trade depended greatly on the high-quality products of its weaving mills. In 1763 a process was even patented that made it possible to weave and quilt on a loom. The patterns were Indian, French, and especially Marseilles quilts. The process consisted of putting a double warp on a power loom which, including an inlay of carded shorn wool, was united according to a pattern by always having a thread from the back come out on the front as "embroidery". The result was a soft, patterned fabric with a three-dimensional appearance, a finer front and somewhat coarser

5 Yellow satin dress from England, quilted after Chinese embroidered patterns, late 19th Century. Victoria and Albert Museum, London.

6 Linen quilt with silk embroidery from England, 1703. Victoria and Albert Museum, London.

back. Within twenty years these woven Marseilles quilts gained a significant place in English textile production, and many of them were sold to America.[7]

Until about 1750, the usually white English quilts were decorated with colored silk embroidery (#6). After the middle of the century, the more economical patchwork became more and more popular as a colorful decoration for quilts. But the course of history shows that it was obviously not possible to give really new impulses to the quilting technique in and of itself. Until today, quilts of one solid color, so-called "wholecloth quilts", have been and are being made, and even being regarded as every quilter's finest work. But the outstanding position of the quilt was reached only through its full development with patchwork, above all in the folk art of North America.

Quilts were normally filled with carded wool or cotton. But one often had to make do with much simpler materials. Feathers, leaves and straw were also suitable, though they had to be changed often. One often finds old wool clothing with its seams separated and ironed out; even old woolen socks were used as quilt filling in very poor households. Pieces of thin wool blankets, as well as thin flannel, also produced a warm quilt. In England the bedclothes of social institutions such as poorhouses and orphanages were filled with paper sewn into cotton bags—which explains why Oliver Twist's patchwork quilt crackled![8]

7 Man's quilted cap from northern Germany, 19th Century. Museum of Art and Craft, Hamburg, West Germany.

Patchwork

Patchwork means nothing else than sewing small pieces of cloth to and on each other. In translating the English word into German, one could call the technique "Flickwerk" or "Lappenarbeit", as is customary for the early work of this kind in the German language area. Toward the end of the Nineteenth Century, the term "Mosaikarbeit" (mosaic work) also became popular; it was intended to make clear the difference between patchwork and the applique technique. In English the definition "patchwork" includes the technique of "pieced work": the work of putting pieces together as well as that of applique. In this book I would like, for the sake of better understanding, to use the word "patchwork" for "pieced work" or "mosaic work" while calling applique by its own name. This is a concession to the German language and not a misunderstanding of otherwise accepted definitions.

Rind and husk fabrics, felt, textiles of wool, silk and plant fibers, leather and fur have been used in patchwork. The choice depended on what was available to those who did the work. It was usually made of worn-out rags and leftover scraps of textiles for very demanding use in everyday life. It fulfilled its purpose again as a bedcover, hanging or piece of clothing until it was finally worn to pieces.

Fortunately, a few historically important witnesses have survived their own times and cultures, and can serve as guides through the necessarily very incompletely recorded history of patchwork. These individual pieces, of course, cannot lead us to draw any great conclusions. One must see them as solitary survivors of an originally very complex and inclusive tradition of patchwork textiles. Only repeatedly appearing and preserved patchworks with common techniques and contents, originating from a single region, let us draw far-reaching conclusions. They help us to fill the gaps, little by little, in the history of patchwork.

An Egyptian canopy quilt from 980 B.C. is generally regarded as the oldest surviving example of antique patchwork. It was used on festive occasions by an Egyptian queen, and consists of squares of dyed gazelle leather sewn together and decorated with symbols. Badly damaged in places, this quilt is preserved today in the Egyptian Museum in Cairo (#8).[9]

8 *Egyptian canopy quilt of gazelle leather, circa 980 B.C., Egyptian Museum, Cairo, Egypt.*

9 *Chinese picture scroll from the 14th Century, unknown artist, 76.5 x 36. The legendary Taoist figure Lan Ts'ai-ho is portrayed. He is said to have appeared often in market places, begging and singing. When he was portrayed later in the theater, his traditional garb, a patchwork coat, was used to characterize him. Museum of East Asiatic Art, Cologne, West Germany.*

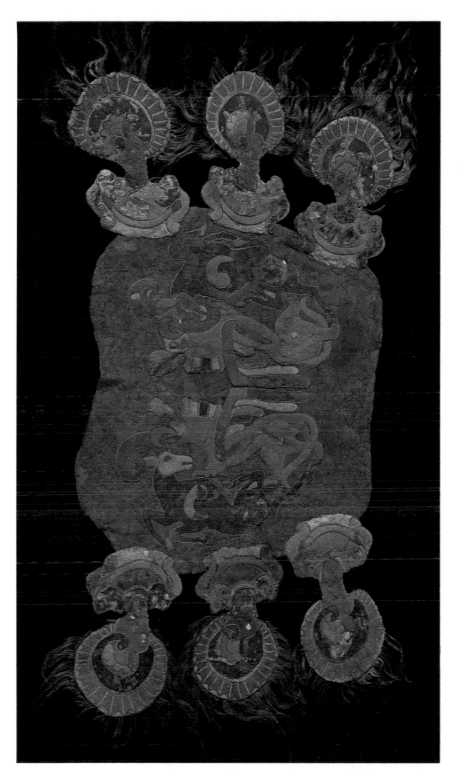

*10 Saddle blanket with felt applique, from the Altai Mountains, Kurgan
I of Pazyryk, 5th Century B.C., 119 x 60. State Hermitage, Leningrad,
USSR.*

Some three hundred years newer are the textiles, decorated with applique, from the excavations of Pazyryk in Central Asia. These hill graves of several tribal chiefs, dating back to the Altai nomadic culture of the 6th to 4th Centuries B.C., have preserved, under the extreme climatic conditions of permafrost, even easily decaying materials such as leather, fur, felt and textiles in a remarkable state of completeness. The example of a saddle blanket, with applique figures of fighting animals, illustrates the Altai people's sense of color and ornamental decoration. The figures of felt show primarily those animals that, as the nomads imagined, were blessed with supernatural powers that protected man (#10).[10]

In the Cave of the Thousand Buddhas, located on the Silk Road in the Serinda region of India, the expedition of Sir Aurel Stein discovered at the beginning of our century a very inclusive collection of costly textiles from the 6th to 9th Centuries. Among them were altar hangings of patterned rectangular pieces of cloth, sewn in patchwork style (#11). The individual pieces were probably votive offerings of travelers who spontaneously tore the pieces out of their clothing. Patchwork banners and a small silk bag, made of squares and triangles, probably used to protect relics, were also found. Sir

11 Silk hanging of votive fragments, 6th-9th Century, Cave of the Thousand Buddhas, Berinda region, India. Calico Museum of Ahmedabad, India.

Aurel Stein's report suggests that this patchwork could have been done by the priests of the holy shrine.[11] Patchwork has played an important role in Buddhism to the present. Patchwork garlands of donated cloth are seen in many temples, where they are supposed to drive evil spirits away. Now and then the monks receive leftover scraps of cloth, as alms, to make their clothes.[12] An expression from China, the term "po-na i", has survived, meaning a monk's habit made of patches. Literally translated, it describes "something made of a hundred patches" (#9).[13]

Asia is generally regarded as the cradle of patchwork and applique. But in Africa and other parts of the world, even today, we find textiles worked in the same manner. They are used for all purposes, as shown by tents and flags, hangings, blankets, wrappings, pillows, bags and clothing from a wide variety of lands prove. Under what conditions and influences the richness of patchwork traditions developed has not yet been determined sufficiently. As a way of utilizing bits and pieces of worn clothing in an economical as well as hard-wearing substitute for laboriously made and costly embroidery, they played a very pragmatic roll in many cultures. But aside from the aspects of utility and decoration, they are often laden with symbolic and magical contents: as religious signs in Buddhism and Islam, or in connection with shamanistic magic. These relationships, too, still need a thoroughgoing explanation of a not merely hypothetical character.

Patchwork and Applique on Tents

Limited technical possibilities are the main reason for the use of patchwork techniques in the making of nomads' tents. The Bedouin women weave narrow strips of cloth made of spun goat's, sheep's and camel's-hair wool on primitive folding looms. These are sewn together by groups of women as communal work, making large rectangles that are later used as tent cloths. The status and wealth of the tent's owner can be read in the length and number of the cloth panels used.[14] Since a tent lasts as long as its "tent family", it must be repaired and patched during the course of time, and so life adds an additional patchwork pattern to it. Many tents are made by this basic principle, even though the procedures vary among different populations. The composition of colors and shapes plays an important role in the case of Saudi Arabian Bedouin tents.[15] The leather tents of the Tuareg, whose women also make very beautiful and colorful utilitarian objects of leather patchwork and applique, also belong in the class of nomad tents whose patchwork grew out of technical necessity. They sew the skins of sheep and goats together into large covers with an awl and leather thongs.[16]

On the other hand, applique was usually added as decoration. In this respect, one could mention the round felt yurts of the Kirghiz nomads as an example. Simple geometrical patterns on hangings decorate doorways and transitions from roof to wall in particular, with a very symbolic significance in protecting these "sensitive" parts of their dwellings.[17]

The appliques of Osmanli-era Turkish tents have a purely decorative character. In the literature these tents are interpreted as direct transitions from Osmanli architectural forms, allowing an extension of social and religious life into dwellings while using the same rules. We cannot get into a discussion here of whether the chronology should be adjusted according to the old rule, "first the tent and then the house"-though it still strikes me as an important consideration. The applique motifs find parallels in the glazed tiles and incrustations that are an important element of Osmanli interior architecture. Normally, the costly Turkish tents were set up not only during military campaigns, but also outside the palace for festive

12 Osmanli tent with decorative applique elements, late 17th Century; silk panel 181 x 818; roof circumference 1590 (excerpt). Museum on the Wavel, Krakau, Poland.

events in peacetime. Presumably the earliest evidence of a tentmakers' guild comes from the time of Mehmed II (1444-1481). Later, with growing need caused by military campaigns, their numbers surely increased. They had to sew and embroider the tents, as well as being responsible for their transport, interior furnishing and repairs.[18] The use of applique technique was especially suited to repair work. It was not only quicker than embroidery but also less laborious. A hole or tear could be covered by sewing on part of a pattern, without making it look obviously like a mend.

During the Turkish wars of the Seventeenth Century, many Turkish tents came into the possession of European princes. Most of them, though, were either destroyed or lost during later campaigns. An example that was preserved is the Turkish booty of "Turk Louis", the Margrave Ludwig Wilhelm of Baden. The greater part of it came from the battle of Salankamen on August 19, 1691 (#13). These treasures, preserved in the Badisches Landes museum in Karlsruhe, West Germany, include a fragment of a decorated tent. Flower patterns of colored silk taffeta and gilded leather were applied to a basic material of satin pieces in various colors, sewn together.[19]

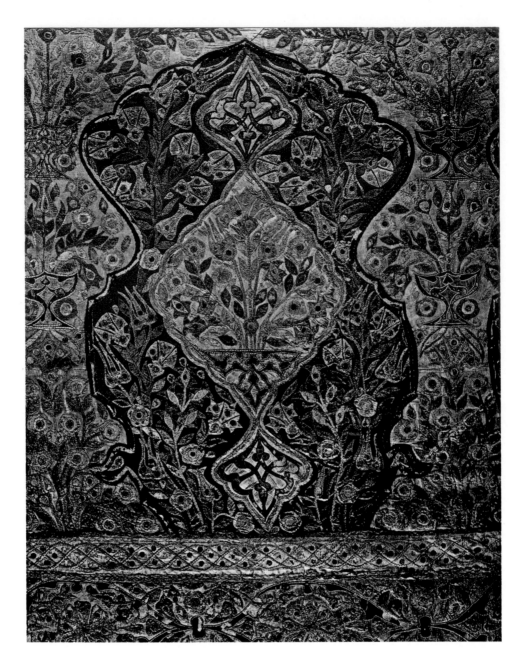

13 Fragment of a Turkish decorated tent from the late 17th Century. Karlsrhue, West Germany.

The Polish Turkish booty from the siege of Vienna in 1683 is now in Warsaw and Krakau (#12). Among this collection is a tent of dyed linen, to which floral designs were applied in linen, leather and satin. During the Eighteenth Century in Poland, military tents were made that copied the Turkish originals and became very popular.[20]

14 Illustrated bible from the Pantheon, Roman school, 12th Century. In the second picture from the top, "Moses and his people set up their tents in the desert of Sinai". Vatican Library, Rome, Italy. (Ms. Vat. Lat. 12858 c.60.v)

Tent cloths with very decorative applique ornamentation are also found in Egypt. The historical background of these panels, known as "Chiameya", has not been thoroughly explained to this day. Kurt Zipper referred to a passage in the Second Book of Moses, in which the building of a dwelling is mentioned. In the 25th Chapter it is enumerated what the Lord asked as a sacrifice from the Children of

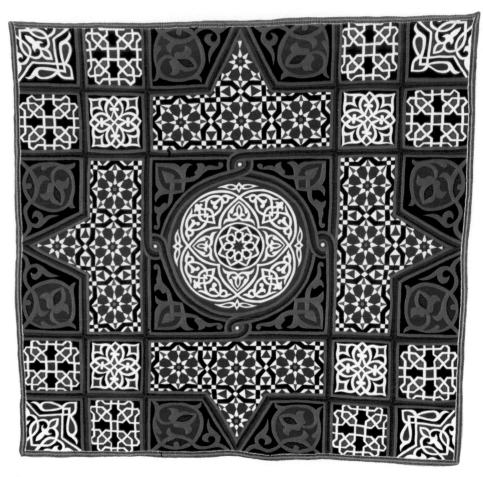

15 Chiameya, Egyptian tent carpet, 264 x 260. German Textile Museum, Krefeld-Linn.

Israel, among other things, blue and red purple, scarlet, costly white linen, goat's hair, reddish ram's skins, badger pelts and much more. In the 26th Chapter, the building of a dwelling "of ten carpets of twined linen, of blue and red purple and of scarlet" is described.[21] In following texts, numerous other biblical passages refer to "embroidered costly linen from Egypt",[22] which perhaps at least allow the hypothesis that the "Chiameya" could have a very long tradition.

In the Second book of Moses, Chapter 19:2, it is reported that Moses and his people set up their tents in the desert of Sinai. This biblical text was illustrated, for example, in a pictorial bible of the Twelfth Century,[23] in a way that it must have required an exact description of Egyptian tents (#14). We know from the depiction of animals how imaginatively the painting monks handled the descriptions of exotic animals that they had never seen with their own eyes. The situation

28

could have been similar with the Egyptian tents, every one of which would fit the description of "colorful" and "ornamentally patterned", even though the "Chiameya" in reality are very different from the portrayal in the illustrated bible. Finally, these hints could be only suggestions meant to shed some light on the unknown history of these tent carpets. Today they are manufactured only in Cairo and used by the local population for all imaginable festive occasions (#15). They are also put to very decorative use as sunshades on open terraces. "Chiameya" are made of undyed white linen, to which bright arabesque-oriental designs of colored cotton cloth are applied according to patterns drawn on beforehand.[24] Under the influence of growing tourism, draperies with ancient Egyptian pharaonic patterns have also been developed. Very large examples of this sort, dating from around 1900, are found in many European collections.[25]

Symbolic West African Appliques

A very special matter apart is the applique material used in the West African state of Dahomey, which reflect the political conditions of the country in a centuries-old tradition. Their production was a monopoly of the court tailors' guild in the capital city of Abomey, who worked under orders from, and followed the imagination of, whoever ruled at the time. The kings of the Alladahonu dynasty, dethroned by the French in 1892, ruled for more than two hundred years. They were the final political, military and judiciary authorities in the country. The regular annual war against one of their neighbor countries was an expression of their aggressive policy of expansion. Their prisoners were sold in a very lucrative slave trade, which was also effective in disciplining their own people. Court ceremonies preceded and followed the annual campaign. Festival tents, ceremonial screens, large coverings and banners on which the heroic deeds of the wars were illustrated in applique work, were important constituents of these festivals (#16). In Forbes,[26] "Dahomey and the Dahomans", of 1851, a carmine red tent-shaped pavilion, twelve meters high, that marked the seat of the king, is described and depicted. The cloth of which it was made was imported from England and decorated with emblems of human skulls and ox heads. Symbols of power were the main theme of the courtly applique art. Battle scenes, executions, symbolic portrayals of the kings in the form of animals or particular objects associated with them, decorated all

16 Applique work from Dahomey: fighting warriors with a lion (King Glele), 19th Century, height 220. Muse/e des Arts Africains et Oceaniens, Paris, France.

the textiles used in these ceremonies. These appliques, in exposed places, transmitted the message of power and death and were classified by the rulers as important instruments of their ruling power. For this reason they kept a strict watch on their production and use.[27]

When the French took power in 1892, the political conditions changed completely. The tailors worked for the new ruling class just as they had previously served the kings, but with the difference that the symbolism of the appliques no longer had an immediate relevance, but only a historical one. Through the changed conditions they gained new circles of customers such as officers and travelers. After Dahomey's independence in 1960, this once so elitist art, rooted in the regional culture, turned to lapidary folkloristic goods for export. Slowly but surely the themes of the appliques changed too. The tailors of today, for the most part, no longer have any spiritual relationship to the picture writing that once used to be understood by all and was often interpreted by accompanying songs. Only the older tailors are able to interpret the symbols now. The preparation of the appliques has declined more and more to the level of a dispassionate mass production.[28]

During colonial times, the applique materials took on an important new meaning in Dahomey, in that they were used in the customary burial rituals. Symbolically represented proverbs decorated the banners brought to a burial. They were explained in song during the ceremony by the adherents of the deceased.[29]

A very similar role was played by the burial cloths of the Anang-Ibibio people in southeastern Nigeria (#17). They were usually made with an applique middle field and a patchwork border, and were stretched over the wooden frames of the burial chambers. The appliques illustrated the life history of the deceased, and were explicated during the burial ceremony by the next of kin. It is not known whether it was customary to prepare the burial cloths in this way with, for example, raffia weaving, before the introduction of printed cotton cloth. Since they were left unprotected to the mercy of the elements after the ceremony, no old examples have survived.

In this respect, it also seems interesting that all the utensils buried with the deceased were made unusable during the ceremony before they were put into the chamber. The intention was probably to make them worthless to plunderers, and that may well have been the reason why the dead-houses were not covered with intact lengths of cloth. To be sure, there was in that region a brotherhood of witch doctors, "ekong kamba", who dressed themselves in patchwork burial cloths for their nocturnal orgies.

The burial ritual described here was suppressed by the growing Christianity, and the patchwork textiles have no more significance in this region.[30].

17 *Burial chamber cloths of the Anang Ibibio, southeastern Nigeria. Oron Museum, Cross River State, Nigeria.*

Asiatic Patchwork Traditions

The making and use of patchwork and applique textiles are often connected with festive events and ceremonies around the world. Trying to describe all the forms of their appearance in these pages would be too much. The richest and most varied traditions relevant to our theme can be found in the north of India, on the peninsula of Kathiawar (Gujarat), in the Kutch region and around Ahmedabad and Bombay. Weddings obviously offer the most important occasions to use textiles with patchwork and applique decorations as parts of the dowry or as decorations.

Patchwork quilts are indispensable components of many brides' dowries, as can be seen in the following example. The peoples of the Kutch region of India, whose ancestors are said to have emigrated from the borderlands between Iran and Iraq some five hundred years ago, are known by the term "Jat". The various tribes are very conscious of their group identity, and their sense of unity is based on their common traditions and their belief in common ancestors. They are Moslems almost without exception, and practice the same wedding customs. Their whole lives are ruled by tradition, and a wedding is to them a significant ritual in which to celebrate this continuity. The dowry is the most important sign of the tradition to which they feel obligated, and whose preservation seems to assure survival. Along with the "Churi", a caftanlike dress with embroidered breast insert, quilts, bags and pillows are essential parts of the dowry (# 18). The quilts are special documents of family and social position within the group. They are made mainly of scraps of worn-out clothes, which in turn indicate by their colors the status and tribal membership of their wearer. The patchwork patterns also are determined by transmitted traditions. Sometimes the geometrical pieces of cloth, squares, rectangles and triangles, are applied to a new or used background which is either made up of pieces itself or even newly dyed. The backs of the quilts are usually made of dark green or black cloth. On their edges and corners, the quilts are decorated with rows of white triangles and rectangles on a red background. When a woman makes her quilt alone, she chooses a pattern of concentrically arranged squares. If several women work on a quilt together, it is

18 Quilt from the Kutch region, "Atree", as a cover for dishes. Museum of Cultural History, Los Angeles, USA.

patterned with parallel lines of patchwork. In both cases the colors of the quilting thread alternate between red and black. Few groups have more deliberately chosen quilt patterns of their own, and individual patchwork and applique patterns deviating from tradition also occur very rarely.[31]

Quilts are made in similarly defined ways in Kathiawar. Used clothes are gathered in a bundle until enough material is at hand to make a new quilt. Torn scraps and rags are made into padding, while the better pieces are used for the front and back of the quilt. The largest and most durable pieces of cloth go in the middle, where, as experience teaches, they are subjected to the most stress. Patchwork and applique complement each other in forming the pattern. Square, rectangular and diamond shapes are sewn on and beside each other. In addition, flower, leaf and cross motifs are appliqued in the middle and along the edges. When the quilt is finished, it is stored in a quilt bag likewise made of patchwork with a decorative border of triangles.

19 Patchwork quilt from the Sindh, Pakistan, "Sindh-Relli", 207 x 125. Auction House of Dr. Fritz Nagel, Stuttgart, West Germany.

20 Patchwork quilt from Amritsar, with excerpt also showing the back, 19th Century, 195 x 115. Museum of Anthropology, Berlin, West Germany.

21 Uzbek Koraki, 58 x 57. Privately owned by Adolf Siegrist, Basel, Switzerland.

The stack of these quilt bags in the storeroom of every house is colorful and eye-catching, and says much about the social position of the possessor. The work of sewing quilts, in which old clothes are torn up to make something new and useful, is seen by the women as a new creation after destruction, a symbolic act in the sense that something dead is reawakened to life.

The quilts are used chiefly as floor coverings or camp-bed mattresses, where they are spread out to sit or lie on. Men and women are allowed to sit on quilts that are white on both sides and decorated at most with a few appliques. Quilts that are made exclusively of colorful women's clothes are reserved for the use of women. Quilts with one white and one colored side can be used by men or women, as long as the correct side is upward (#20).[32]

The traditional use of patchwork quilts is naturally also seen in other regions. They scarcely differ in their appearance, which is dominated by simple geometric patterns. Only the applique quilts of the Mahajan area are truly unique. Here the quilts are decorated with strictly geometrical negative appliques. The pattern is cut out of brightly-colored cloth that has been folded several times, just as patterns are cut in paper, and is actually seen only when the white applique background is shimmering through. [33]

Very similar patterns with negative appliques are seen in the quilts of the Sindh, who live in West Pakistan (#19). They are made through the joint efforts of the women within a family, and are used mainly as blankets for outdoor sleeping. Their patterns—which Westerners may compare with the variety of snowflake shapes—are meant to reflect the starlit skies. Small pattern squares cover the surfaces of the quilts evenly or in checkerboard patterns, alternating with squares of one color. From the central Sindh, on the other hand, comes very colorful work in black, red, yellow and white. Strictly geometrical patchwork quilts also come from this region.[34]

Patchwork textiles turn up throughout Asia as festive decorations. Colorful horse and ox blankets as well as "Osmolduks", camel flank hangings, and elephant decorations are a bright part of many ceremonies and festivals (#22). In place of once widespread embroidery, colorful appliques are seen, their designs based only on the old embroidery patterns, their effect resembling that of placards. The combination of patchwork, applique and embroidery is often seen as well. The colors red, white, black and yellow dominate this style in all textiles, even pure patchwork. Those draperies and covers in which the quilted squares are attached to each other only at the corners could be called a kind of pierced work. They lie like a "net" of diamonds over the pelt of an animal and let it shine through. Silk and cotton materials are preferred, usually given by family members and friends on the occasion of, for example, a wedding. In addition, the front hall and veranda of the house are decorated with wall hangings on a wedding day. In Kathiawar these consist of a frieze (pachhitpati) showing gods and processional scenes similar to those carved in stone in Hindu and Jain temples. Square pattern fields made of patchwork diamonds are attached to them. The pierced work described above is also used for wall hangings.

22 Uzbek camel flank hanging (diamond net), 155 x 110. Privately owned by Adolf Siegrist, Basel, Switzerland.

Square wrapping cloths of patchwork and applique, in which portions of the dowry or gifts were wrapped, can also be hung up as wall decoration.[35] These textiles are related to Afghan Korakis and Korean wrapping cloths in both appearance and use. The geometry of the patterns is varied only by the different choice of fabrics in the various countries (# 21).

It is known that Afghan Korakis are made with symbolic patterns and colors: they are supposed to keep demons and evil spirits away. Yellow repels ghosts, white works against the evil eye. Green, the color of nature, is the sacred color, and red is dedicated to Mohammed. The triangle is the Turkmen protective sign, and the eight-pointed star stands for Solomon, prophet of the Moslems. Five squares combined in a pointed symbol curse everything that could harm a nomad woman. The embroidered tribal symbol or a lock of hair wrapped in silk indicate the personal reference and the relation to symbols of shamanistic belief.[36] A similar type of symbolism is quite imaginable for the wrapping cloths of India.

The concept that patches turn away evil seems to speak for the use of patchwork textiles in religious festivals and ceremonies. But in addition to quilts and draperies, many useful things have been made of patchwork and applique all over Asia. The generally very simple and yet colorful patterns are made of the widest variety of fabrics and qualities, from simple cotton to luxurious ikats, silks and brocades. The involvement of these textiles in traditions is being made increasingly questionable by continuing social change, so that they may soon be merely a part of cultural history.

23 Jacket and skirt as wedding clothes of the Black Miao, Guizhow, China. Museum für Völkenkunde, Berlin, West Germany.

Patchwork and Applique to Decorate Clothing

The decoration of clothing with patchwork, and especially with applique, has been widespread among all peoples at all times. Here too, they offer advantages over the more sensitive embroidery. The material is too vast, though, to allow us to describe every patchwork and applique "style" here. So let us again choose a few examples which will show us at least a part of the variety.

The work with which the people of northern Russia and the Kamchatka Peninsula decorate their clothes and covers is known as pelt mosaic. Pieces of pelts in contrasting colors are cut into geometric pieces and sewn together so that a dark pattern on a light background, or a light pattern on a dark background, results. Rhythmically alternating small triangles, small rectangles in zigzag patterns, and the most varied combinations of squares and diamonds form stripes of patterns and fields that are usually set on the shoulder yokes, seams and sleeve joints of parkas and anoraks (# 24). One can scarcely imagine the unbelievably fine handiwork with which the basically very obstinate material is combined to form tiny and neatly worked patterns. Since the color essentially depends on the contrast of light and dark pelts, and can be brightened at best with piping and edging of red, blue or yellow wool material, these patterns are known to the local people as "northern light patterns".[37]

Especially intricate, colorful and very decorative appliques and patchwork are sewn by the women of the Hmong, Miao, Lahu, Akha and Lisu. These tribal groups live chiefly in southwestern China and the southern parts of central China today, as well as in the northern parts of Thailand, Laos and Vietnam. They have mastered a richness of textile techniques to a particular degree, with embroidery and applique the most important of them (#23).

The variety of applique and patchwork forms in their clothing and household textiles really makes a general description impossible. On the other hand, a too thorough differentiation at this point would go too far. The fabrics used are woven out of hand-spun hemp or cotton yarn or bought from traveling peddlers. Red, blue, black and white dominate, amplified by a very bright and effective array of colors. Stripes and triangles are sewn together in patchwork technique, to decorate the sleeves of jackets and blouses as well as the boot-tops or

24 Korjak winter coat, Kamchatka, Siberia, 19th Century. Museum für Völkenkunde, Berlin, West Germany.

Detail of "northern light pattern" from the winter coat in #24.

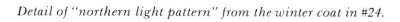

leggings that are a part of almost all feminine attire. The appliques are basically limited to geometric forms, especially triangles and squares, plus a limited assortment of floral patterns. Negative appliques, in which two layers of different-colored cloth are overlaid, are most popular. The cutout patterns allow the underlying color to show through. The motifs are further contrasted by the addition of white borders or embroidery, which serve to make the already very fine and intricate work even more distinctive.

In almost all tribal groups, the marriageable young people wear the most elaborate clothing. With great ambition, the young girls spend much time on the preparation of their clothing, which generally consists of a jacket or blouse, a pleated skirt or trousers, leggings, scarf, neckcloth or apron as well as a head covering. "In the hope of being able to increase their desirability to girls, the mothers devote just as great care to the dressing of their sons."[38] The most beautiful pieces of clothing are worn to celebrate the new year, since it is feared that wearing old clothes at this time could lead to poverty in the new year.

Children's caps and baby wrappings are also lovingly decorated with striking, artistic negative appliques. The various stages of growing up, divided by certain festivals, are documented by changes in clothing and outfitting. Wedding clothes once again have an outstanding importance. Even the dead are dressed splendidly before they are buried. In every case there are enough opportunities for the women to work with great care on the preparation of the traditional tribal costumes.[39]

The Ainu, original inhabitants of Japan, who live as fishers and hunters on the island of Hokkaido, have for centuries decorated their clothing with nothing other than applique and embroidery (#25). It is probable that the applique technique of this entire group of people was developed technically from leather patchwork. Since the earliest times, clothing, gloves, bags and other articles have been made by sewing various large fish skins and animal pelts together. Different colors and textures automatically formed the loveliest patchwork patterns. The tradition of such leather work can be traced back several centuries farther than the use of woven textiles. The use of a type of buttonhole embroidery in the appliques forms the technical relationship with these early leather patchworks.

Scientists have related the Ainu patterns to Jomon string ceramics. That means that their formal origins and symbolic content can be traced back to the Third Century B.C. Just as the patterns of Jomon ceramics are presumably meant to protect the contents of containers from poison and spoilage, these bands of ornamentation on Ainu clothing, always symmetrically arranged, protect the wearer's body from illness and injury. The appliques are usually applied only to the necklines or down the backs, along seams, sleeves and cuffs, since the openings must be protected particularly by magical patterns. A pattern covering the entire piece of clothing is found only in a few regions of Hokkaido. The Ainu patterns must be regarded as a synthesis of Jomon ornamentation—inspired by shamanism—and foreign, especially Chinese influences. They have been sewn onto textiles only by women, and have retained their original form most of all there, in comparison to all other realms of artistic handicraft. The oldest surviving textiles produced by the Ainu themselves come from the late Eighteenth and early Nineteenth Centuries. Since 1912 they have, to be sure, lost much of their authenticity.

The fabrics woven by the Ainu on very primitive looms out of fibers of atusi bark were supplemented by the importing of cotton, silk and ramie from Honshu and China. The imported textiles seem to have included not only cloth but also finished articles of clothing such as kimonos, coats and theatrical costumes, which were particularly popular. Even so, they do not seem to have influenced the original native style of dress significantly. Only when they were torn and worn were they cut up and applied to Ainu clothing in traditional spiral or labyrinth patterns, additionally decorated with sparing embroidery.[40]

The patchwork and applique of the Edo period (from the Seventeenth to the Nineteenth Century) have been called "kirihame" in Japan, even when these techniques had been utilized long before (#26). "Kirihame" can be traced back as clothing decoration to the year 1056 under the name "zogan", which is only applied to wood or metal inlay work today. In that year an article of clothing with a blue "zogan" pattern on a white background was described as having been worn by a participant in the New Year poetry competition in the palace of the Empress.[41]

During the Edo period a costume tradition developed that was based on the use of "kirihame", that is, patchwork and applique. Most of all, Kosode and Noh costumes, made of several different pieces of cloth, took the form of "katami hawari" kimonos. These garments let us trace a regular development from strict to very free patchwork designs. The first step led to cutting two kimonos in halfs and then combining the four halves again to make two new garments with different parts. This was also a useful way to go on using the useful half of a kimono if the rest was spoiled. It seems doubtful, to be sure, that such economic aspects would have played a role here, for these garments were worn exclusively by very wealthy and prestigious personalities. One must assume that this principle was followed mainly for esthetic reasons. In this respect one might mention the tradition of paper collage, as shown, for example, in the Sanjuroko-nin Kashu Anthology at the Nishi Hongan-ji Temple in Kyoto, from

25 Ainu outer garment of the inner bark of the atsui tree, with appliques and embroidery, 19th Century, Japan. Museum für Völkerkunde, Berlin, West Germany.

26 Kosode costume from Japan, circa 1700. Example of patterns developed from the kirihame technique. Deutsches Textile Museum, Krefeld-Linn, West Germany.

27 Leather patchwork garment of a Liberian chief. Front and back. Ethnographic Museum, Oslo, Norway.

the first half of the Twelfth Century. Pieces of paper in various colors and shapes were cut and combined in an endless variety of variations and ever-new forms. After the vertical division of the garment, following this principle of formation, there followed the horizontal division, and then the combination of both types into a large-surface checkerboard pattern called "dan-gawari". Above and beyond this there developed a richness of free patterns, arranged geometrically as patchwork or running organically as appliques. The individual

46

28 Fur coat for a woman, from northern Slovakia, with applique and pelt mosaic, front and back, end of the 19th Century. Museum für Völkenkunde, Berlin, West Germany.

29 *Mola of the Cuna Indians with negative applique, San Blas Islands, Panama. Privately owned by Christoph Schmidt, Hamburt, West Germany.*

patterns are always made to achieve a harmonious effect, and the assumption that the "kirihame" techniques were used only for esthetic reasons becomes clear. Embroidery and textile printing were also used for the sake of effect (# 26).[42]

Patchwork clothing as a privilege of the ruling class, however anachronistic that may strike us, is found again and again, not only in Asia but also in West and North Africa. Chiefs of the Asante and Wuinta of Ghana wore robes of patchwork and applique, so that they were acknowledged as "greatest". Liberia provides the example of leather patchwork garments that were worn by chiefs at the beginning of our century (#27a, b).[43] This aspect will be taken up again later.

The thesis cannot be mainained that patchwork and applique could be regarded as synonymous with poverty and destitution because they were merely the art of "patching". On the contrary, all cultures in which patchwork and applique textiles traditionally occur have regarded them as bearing special social, religious or at least decorative symbols.

48

It does not matter at all whether they are "mouse-tooth" appliques, rows of small white triangles on the jackets and vests of the women of Celebes and the Moluccas,[44] or the felt and leather appliques on the coats of East Europeans (#28a, b).[45] Whether they are the varied "molakana" of the Cuna Indians from the San Blas Islands (#29)[46] or the simple patchwork cloaks of the black people of Surinam[47]—they all have more than a decorative significance. Was Yves Saint Laurent aware of this when he once designed a patchwork wedding gown[48] for a French noblewoman?

Symbolic Power of Patchwork Clothing

As an outward sign of their vow of poverty, Buddhist and Moslem monks, fakirs and dervishes have always worn patchwork cloaks, robes and mantles (#30). The Dervishes described Mohammed as a man who always wore patched clothing, and his successors, the "four justly commanding caliphs", did the same. It was reported of Caliph Omar that he often slept beside the poor people on the steps of the mosque. It happened that emissaries from distant provinces had to search diligently for the "ruler of the faithful" and were very amazed to find him in a patchwork robe. But how impressed the emissaries must have been![49]

The Dervishes, organized into sects and orders, tried through prayer, song and worldly poverty to attain a mystic unity with their creator. At the same time they were highly educated and appeared as teachers and wise men. Again and again in reports of travels in Persia and Central Asia one finds descriptions of the Dervishes in patchwork clothing, which singled them out and marked them as wise and pious men.

30 Dervish coat from Persia, mid-19th Century. Museum of für Völkenkunde, Berlin, West Germany.

Around the middle of the 19th Century, the members of the Dervish order of Samarija gathered around Mohammed Ahmed, who claimed to be the Mahdi prophesied by the Prophet. As "Mahdists" they rose up in Kordofan in 1881 against the Egyptian government. They wore genuine patchwork uniforms, and their officers had very elegant-looking white uniform coats with brown and blue appliques (#31). After several victories gained between 1881 and 1883, the Mahdists came to power in Kordofan, as was recognized by the English governor in Khartoum. Thus they ruled over the eastern Sudan and were able to maintain this power under the Mahdi's successor, Abdullahi ibn Seji Mohammed, until 1898. Only then were the English under Lord Kitchener able to regain the eastern Sudan.[50]

The wearing of patchwork and quilted armor in Africa was obviously nothing out of the ordinary, as is proved by several Nineteenth-Century reports, of which we shall cite two here as examples.

From Ghana comes the interesting description of a battle-dress that was sent to the King of England by the Asanti leader in 1820 as part of a large collection of gifts. It was a kind of cotton robe, partially

31 Uniform jacket of a Mahdi officer, eastern Sudan, end of the 19th Century. Museum für Völkenkunde, Berlin, West Germany.

51

32 Quilted horse armor from the Sudan. Museum of Mankind, London, UK.

covered with mysterious scraps of cloth and Arabic lettering. As armor, it could withstand the recoil of a flintlock gun just as well as a blow with a steel weapon.[51] The Batakaraki chiefs wear this type of clothing, the use of which certainly originated among the Asanti leaders, today as part of their insignia of state.[52]

On his travels through North and Central Africa from 1849 to 1855, the German explorer Heinrich Barth once accompanied the mounted army, numbering several thousand men, of the ruler of Bornu, on a campaign against a neighboring principality. "The horses wore thick quilted armor of kapok wadding, which protected them against swords, arrows and spears. The riders were dressed in coats of the same material" (#32).[53]

In 1984 a great-grandson of the Sultan of Zinder, still wearing the same kind of outfit, greeted a German expedition.[54]

But one need not stay in Africa to find patchwork as a sign of spiritual or princely power. The Islamic princes of central Java wore patchwork jackets for official functions, showing them to be the highest religious leaders (#33). This "Kyay Antakusuma" (honorable many-flowering) is supposed to have been received by an Islamic holy man as a gift of God. One assumes a magic character of the individual pieces of valuable material. Along with it went a slender

33 Sultan Hamenku Buwono VII of Jakarta (1877-1921) in robes of state with a patchwork jacket. Tropical Museum, Amsterdam.

shawl, "Samir belah ketupat", as the Grand Mistress of Ceremonies' sign of office. Until the end of the last century, the soldiers of the princely bodyguard likewise wore patchwork vests, decorated just like the jacket and the shawl with a windmill pattern of triangles. It must be assumed that these garments originated in pre-Islamic traditions. In Javanese shadow plays, whose repertoire includes the pre-Hindu cult of ancestor worship as well as the old Indian "Ramayana" and "Mahabarata" epics, the "Durna" priest and teacher is always characterized by a patchwork pattern. The ancient Javanese figure of the wise man, "Semar", who appears with his sons as funmakers and advisors of the good party, does not appear in the Indian version of the Mahabarata but also has a loincloth with a patchwork windmill pattern.[55]

Patchwork does not have to, but it can signify power and greatness, symbolically protect against spirits and dangers, and characterize magicians and wise men. Obviously, it is very seldom used purely for decoration.

Patchwork in Europe

The Crusaders have often been made responsible for the introduction of patchwork and applique techniques into Europe. Their cloaks, banners and flags were splendidly decorated with appliqued heraldic devices (#34, 35).

The oldest surviving example of applique work in the German language area, as has been cited over and over in the literature, should be the imperial mantle of St. Kunigunde, which was listed among the treasures of the Bamberg Cathedral in 1010.[56] Since the First Crusade, involving chiefly the French knighthood and the south Italian Normans, took place only in 1096, the Crusaders could scarcely be cited for introducing patchwork to Europe, even though it sounds so plausible. But the fact is that the early medieval silk embroidery of the imperial mantle was cut out and appliqued to a blue satin background only in the Sixteenth Century.[57] It is important to set the facts of this quasi-example straight, because the authors always cite the same more-or-less spectacular stories when writing of the European history of patchwork and applique techniques. In most cases, they offer neither sources of information nor illustrations, and so their assertions remain unprovable, and yet they are dragged through the greater part of the literature.

There are naturally several examples of patchwork in Europe and even more for applique. But one must recognize that these were two of many techniques of textile formation, and they were never very widespread or popular. So we cannot speak of traditions in this area.

Appliques were preferred for the formation of churchly textiles. The literature says that the painter Sandro Botticelli (1444/45-1510) of Florence was the first to introduce appliqued wall hangings into the great Italian churches.[58] This conclusion was probably drawn from the writings of Giorgio Vasari, biographer of artists, who reports that Botticelli prepared plans for "lavori di commesso", contract work. His fellow artists Antonio Pollaiuolo (1431-1498) and Andrea del Sarto (1486-1531) also did this, but only for the then very famous embroidery workshops located in Florence, for they carried out the contract work. They created silk embroidery in needle painting, stitching with gold accents and in the des or nue/ technique, after the plans and colored patterns of the artists. (FN 59) Neither applique nor patchwork was used in the process, and no examples of it have survived.

34 *Great Heidelberg Song Manuscript "Codex Manesse" (Walter von Klingen), early 14th Century. Fighting knights in clothing decorated with patchwork and applique. Unversity Library, Heidelberg (Cod. Pal. Gem. 848, fol52»), West Germany*

35 *Julius Banner of the Province of Saanen, Milan, 1512, 173 x 154. Made of Milanese silk damask with pomegranate patterns, appliqued and embroidered flying crane and figure of Christ. Historical Museum, Bern, Switzerland.*

36 Antependium of the Mariners' Guild of Nijmegen, circa 1494, 220 x 98. Nijmeegs Museum, Commanderie van Sint Jan, Nijmegen, Netherlands.

On the other hand, there are several examples from The Netherlands which show appliques from the same era. An antependium of the Mariners' Guild of Nijmegen, in silk applique undelaid with paper, was created around 1494 (#36).[60] One is inclined to think that such works were not isolated cases.

During the Sixteenth and Seventeenth Centuries, appliqued textiles, also known as intarsia embroidery, can be proved to exist all over Europe. Most of them are churchly articles, from wall hangings to choir gowns. In well-to-do circles they also occurred as draperies, bedcovers and pillows as well as decorations for clothing.

Even crowned heads are said to have occupied themselves with patchwork, and particularly with applique work. Mary Queen of Scots, as a young girl at the French court, learned needlework from Catherine de Medici and was taught to make lace, embroidery and appliques. During her long imprisonment, these abilities are said to have helped her get her mind off her sorrow. Her work can still be seen today in England's Hardwick Hall.

In all the writings of the French Revolution there are reports of a quilt of Queen Marie Antoinette, which the ladies at the court of her mother, Maria Theresia of Austria, are said to have spent eight long years sewing for her. It was carefully decorated with appliques of birds, cupid figures and other symbols of love.[61]

Appliques were sewn in all the countries of Europe, especially Italy, Spain and France, since the Sixteenth Century, mainly of costly materials such as silk, satin, velvet and brocade (#38). Patchwork was made, if at all, in less wealthy circles and in rural areas. The European textiles of this nature seem to have had no great importance in the future development of this technique in England and the United States.

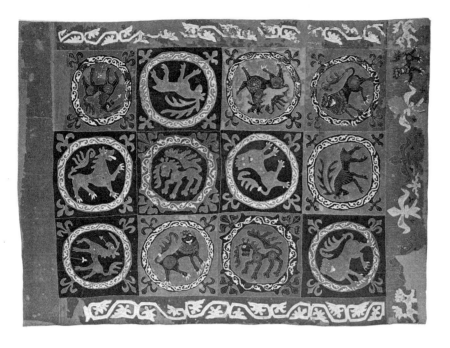

37 Patchwork and applique quilt from Dahlem, Sweden, early 15th Century, 270 x 210. Statens Historica Museer, Stockholm, Sweden.

38 Italian wall hanging with appliques, end of the 16th Century. Victoria and Albert Museum, London, UK.

To my knowledge, the oldest surviving European patchwork quilt is preserved in Sweden, where it was probably made for a wedding in 1303. It shows the comb of a German princess, which has been seen as proof that this technique was introduced from Germany. Also from Sweden is a quilt of the early Fifteenth Century, made of twelve squares sewn together and decorated with intarsia embroidery (#37). Pillows, bedclothes and draperies sewn in this manner were donated to the church after they had first served earthly purposes.[62]

Sewing and Patching Work

In the German language area, many examples of work done by sewing scraps of cloth, and decorated with simple or ornamental embroidery on the background fabric, have survived. These textiles are mentioned in very reliable sources.[63] We find them as pillows in the Vierlande area (#39a, b) and Schleswig-Holstein, as well as so-called comb covers such as were used in East Prussia. Silesian burial cloths and the coffin shields of the Breslau guilds were worked in this same manner. Leather work includes red, green and yellow decorative forms on dark red backgrounds in the covers of Bavarian-Franconian baskets as well as Siebenburg neckcloths, church pelts and men's belts.

Larger applique quilts were made in Lower Saxony during the Fifteenth Century. A portrayal of the legend of Tristan from this era has survived, as has a contemporary wall hanging that shows Jesus'

39 Patchwork pillows from the Vierlande area near Hamburg, 18th-19th Centuries, 50 x 50. Museum für Kunstund Gewerbe, Hamburg, West Germany.

40 Hanging, "Roots of Jesse", from Lower Saxony, end of the 14th Century, 289 x 221. Duke Anton Ulrich Museum, Braunschweig, West Germany.

family tree, the latter from the church in Nordsteimke, near Wolfsburg (#40). Blue cloth forms the background; the border is red. The gold of the appliqued leather strips and the embroidered faces have faded with time.

Hessian "Kopflegen", Schwalm "Kitzel" or Swabian "Bäuschtle" are made by a combination of sewing work and mosaiclike piecing of cloth (#41). These rings of pieced cloth were placed on their heads by farm women to ease the carrying of burdens such as water buckets and

41 *Hessian head pillow. Privately owned by Hans Deibel, Schlitz, West Germany.*

baskets. The upper and lower surfaces of these pillows are pieced together of varicolored, wedge-shaped pieces of cloth and set with cutout cloth designs.

Several splendid patchwork quilts have survived from the Eighteenth Century and could probably represent a more extensive tradition in the region of their origin.

A valuable wall hanging has survived from the Catholic parsonage in Geldern on the Lower Rhine; it probably served as a Lenten "Fastenvelum" for a small cloister church (#42). This patchwork of small and even smaller pieces of cloth portrays in impressive colors the story of Christ's sorrows. Even the finest stripes, letters and rows of flowers are sewn together from behind, edge to edge, in painstaking handwork, without a common background to hold the pieces of cloth. The occasion for this work is explained as follows: "Jacobus Demans and his wife Johanna Magda Ressels, as recorded in the church records of the St. Magdalen Parish in Geldern, were married there on June 7, 1735. On July 6 of the same year, lightning struck the great tower on the Hart Gate in Geldern, in which the powder magazine was located. Great portions of the city were destroyed in the explosion thus caused, and all the churches and cloisters were destroyed. So it may be presumed that theg givers Jacob Demans and Johanna Ressels, whose names can be read on the hanging, gave one of the cloisters the scraps of cloth, perhaps with the suggestion that a decoration for the refectory or for the beautification of the church be made thereof." One must assume that this hanging was a religious-dogmatically related communal project, probably made by the nuns in the Carmelite Cloister of Elzendaal near Boxmeer. The materials

60

include feltlike wool cloth, simple linen weave as well as black and patterned linen, blue-white patterned two-sided weave, patterned velvet and white leather. The back is covered with a light and dark brown piece of calico.

Other than these, only smaller framed patchwork pictures are known from the Lower Rhine area.[64]

A particularly beautiful example of patchwork from the southeast German area was owned by the Görlitz Museum. This quilt, dated 1789, with scenes from the Creation to the Crucifixion of Christ, was unfortunately destroyed in World War II. A patchwork quilt in the same tradition still survives in the City Museum of Bautzen (#43). It is sewn of uniform scraps of cloth and shows chessboard and star patterns, soldiers, Turks, miners, hunters and other patterns. The

42 Hunger cloth from Geldern, mid-18th Century, 210 x 165. Lower Rhine Museum for Ethnography and Cultural History, Kevelaer, West Germany.

43 Patchwork quilt from southeastern Germany, 1776-1779. City Museum, Bautzen, German Democratic Republic.

years 1776 and 1779 may stand for the beginning and end of the work, or could also, considering the themes of the patterns, refer to a political connection. At this time the War of the Bavarian Succession took place, with Prussian troops marching into Bohemia. The Peace of Teschen ended the war in 1779.

In the Victoria and Albert Museum in London there is another Bohemian bedcover from 1796, likewise showing a combination of patchwork and applique (#44). Here rectangular pieces of cloth were sewn together for the background, and on the resulting fields, scenes and figures were appliqued and embroidered. In the center stands a

44 Bedcover from Bohemia, end of the 18th Century. Victoria and Albert Museum, London.

two-headed eagle, surrounded by small scenes and sentry-boxes. Soldiers have taken positions at his feet. The reference to politics of the time and the Turkish wars seems clear.

The patched works described here show an almost naive joy in telling a story in terms of certain thematic portrayals. The purely decorative patterns are especially interesting in view of the applique quilts made by German emigrants such as the Pennsylvania Dutch, who emigrated from Bohemia via The Netherlands to the United States.

Patchwork and Quilts
in 18th-Century England

The oldest surviving patchwork from England was made in 1708, presumably by the second wife of Colonel Sir James Grahme, her stepdaughters and other women at Levens Hall, Westmoreland. It consists of a patchwork quilt and bed hangings sewn out of colorfully printed Indian calico.[65]

In 1700 the import of Indian, Persian and Chinese calico was legally banned. The administration had to take this step under the pressure of the British weavers, who feared the competition with the reasonably priced, colorfully printed cotton fabrics. As a result, ways and means of partially circumventing the ban were found, but the prices of the favored cloth went up sharply. Some importers stated that the calicos and chintzes were to be exported again, which was legal, and unloaded these cargoes on quiet stretches of the English coast. The Eighteenth-Century quilt from Levens Hall shows very clearly how hard people tried to make a useful and decorative everyday object out of a small amount of expensive fabric (#47). The colorfully patterned octagons, diamonds and crosses were sewn to a white background. Some pieces were composed of smaller pieces, a typical sign of how economically the costly material was used. Scraps seem to have been used, for otherwise it would have been possible to cut out colored patterns and applique them to the white background. That would have been at least more "fashionable". This technique was later called "broderie perse" and often used in making quilts. This patchwork, covered with a quilted diamond pattern and sewn with red thread, gives the impression of having been made by highly qualified seamstresses.

It is easy to assume that there was originally more patchwork from this era. A hint may be found in Jonathan Swift's book, "Gulliver's Travels", published in 1726. Gulliver describes the making of his clothes, measured and sewn by three hundred Lilliputian tailors: "It looked like the patchwork made by the ladies in England, except that mine was all one color."[65]

Although there are no other public references from the time before 1750, one may assume that similar quilts to that in Levens Hall were made. Patchwork of wool, linen, cotton and silk fabrics must also be presumed, especially as the laws banning printed fabrics were to become even more stringent.

45 Cotton patchwork quilt, England, 1797. Victoria and Albert Museum, London, UK.

In 1712 high use taxes were set on printed fabrics made in England, and in 1720 the production of all printed cotton textiles except union cloth[66] was banned. In the end none of these laws prevented textiles from being printed, but the development of textile printing was severely retarded. The bans were lifted only in 1774, because the government had recognized that they had failed to achieve their purpose of stifling the demand for printed cloth. In their place, high use taxes were again imposed, and were maintained until 1831.[67]

It seems clear against this background why so little patchwork from the first half of the century has survived. Scarcely any other textile was as durable as calico. One can imagine that patchwork was made, especially by poor people, mainly out of used clothing and scraps. Such simple quilts would be worn out by regular use, so that today more speculations than concrete examples remain. Instead,

46 Formerly called a cotton quilt by Elizabeth Griffith, 1770, now regarded as 19th-Century work. The quilt shows a variety of patterns and possible combinations of them. Victoria and Albert Museum, London.

several quilts decorated with beautiful silk embroidery have survived. Colored thread was obviously easier to obtain than desirable printed cloth, and it may have been simpler to use embroidery as a means of making colorful patterns. Only in the latter half of the Eighteenth Century did embroidery give way more and more to patchwork and applique. So patchwork quilts have survived for the most part from the last twenty years of the century. Almost all of them were sewn of colored cotton prints, fabrics meant for clothing and decorative use. Mosaic patterns in varying shapes and colors, arranged in groups and rows, were combined with embroidery and applique. Most of the quilts, though, show a central motif enclosed by several patterned borders: the so-called "medallion style". The formation of the center was handled with particular care, while the borders were often made of variations of geometric patchwork patterns.

A patchwork quilt dated 1797 shows a wide variety of the patchwork patterns known at that time, even though some of them are not to be found in other work of the same era or only reappeared

66

47 Details of a patchwork bed curtain from Levens Hall, 1708. Levens Hall, Kendal,
UK.

48 Durham Quilt, England, circa 1920, 230 x 200. Privately owned by Barbara and Paul Clemens, Cologne, West Germany.

in other work fifty years later (#45). More than sixty different patterns appear in over two hundred square, rectangular and triangular blocks.[68]

In addition to the often unquilted patchwork bedcovers, there was also a very widespread tradition of pure one-colored quilts (#46). In the West of England these were usually made in geometric patterns formed by straight stitching lines. In America such "all-over" quilt patterns were particularly praised as ideal, understated completions of colorful patchwork articles. On the North Coast of England, quilt patterns were usually developed from natural forms into abstractions,

49 Durham Quilt, England, circa 1920, 230 x 200. Privately owned by Barbara and Paul Clemens, Cologne, West Germany.

while in the South such inspirations from the environment were rendered as true-to-life as possible. In the early quilts, the background is evenly covered with patterns. Later themes were developed for whose formation the principle of the framed medallion played just as important a role as in the design of patchwork and applique bedcovers. The space between the central pattern and the borders was filled in with other patterns. If the center was round, then the space was filled with squares, rectangles and diamonds. If the motif was rectangular or square, then it was surrounded with clamshell or wineglass patterns (#48, 49).[69]

The English Colonies
in North America

The moving accounts of the hard life of the first settlers in the new continent, as told in most books about patchwork quilts, will be replaced here by a brief look at the historical conditions of the first settling of the East Coast of North America.

For England the Sixteenth Century was a time of great social layering. The power of the feudal lords was broken, farmers lost their dependent status—and often their land as well. In the cities, especially London, a rich bourgeoisie developed and gained a weighty influence on the process of government. The resulting wealthy state of the bourgeois middle classes was known throughout Europe, and England's military triumphs over Spain, The Netherlands and France gained great respect all over the world. The levels of society that stimulated the settlement of the new continent were those with capital: the businessmen and property owners who also had experience in governing, as well as craftsmen and farmers driven from their lands. They all looked for new means of existence. Along with economic reasons, political ambition also played a major role in the settlement of North America, especially to establish a new and firm position against their constant enemy, Spain.

The London Company's expedition to Virginia, named after the 'Virgin Queen' Elizabeth, was led by Captain John Smith. In his "History of Virginia"[70] in 1624, he described how carpenters, farmers, gardeners, fishermen, smiths and masons were needed above all in the New World, since one could expect nothing there but what one could gain by his own work. After years of privation, a secure foundation for life was finally found in tobacco growing. As a result there developed in the southern part of North America's East Coast a form of economy and society based on great land possessions and plantation activity. Later the cultivation of sugar cane, indigo and cotton was added, and this system was conducted with the help of slaves in Virginia and other Southern colonies.

The "Pilgrim Fathers", with their famous "Mayflower", landed in New England, in present-day Massachusetts, in 1620, though their original goal had also been Virginia. These Puritans settled in as craftsmen and farmers. Many members of the prosperous English middle class followed them, fleeing from the political and religious disputes of the Stuart kings (1603-1688). Because of the climatic and geological conditions, life in new England was much harder than in Virginia. Village and city communities developed in which people depended on each other, and the land was cultivated by free individual farmers.

The colonies soon spread out to the south and west. The founding of Maryland by the Catholic Lord Baltimore in 1634, and of Pennsylvania by the Quaker William Penn in 1682, and the successful takeover of the Dutch colony of New Amsterdam on the Hudson in 1664 extended them along the entire East Coast. They still belonged to the English crown and were closely linked, both economically and culturally, with the mother country.

Raw materials such as lumber for shipbuilding, grain, furs, tobacco and many others were the principal exports that moved eastward to the Old World. The people in the colonies imported consumer goods such as textiles, furniture, tools, paper, utensils and many others. Textiles of all kinds formed the greatest portion of the imports. In the Seventeenth and Eighteenth Centuries, France, England, Spain, Portugal and Holland competed for the best trade routes in the world, but trade with North America had been, for the most part, monopolized by England through control of the ports and import duties. Beyond that, English dealers bought large amounts of wine, cotton and silk from France, shipped these to the colonies, and made large profits as middlemen. By passing strict laws, England assured itself of the greatest part of this market and could thereby maintain the dependent state of the colonies in every sense.

But in the course of time the interests diverged more and more, all the more so as the colonists were allowed no representation in Parliament, although they had to support its decisions. High taxes were imposed on them to pay for the colonial wars waged by England (for example, that of 1760 against the French colonies of Canada and Louisiana), which was regarded as an injustice. With the help of political support from France, the thirteen colonies, under the leadership of George Washington, finally freed themselves from the English mother country in the Revolutionary War of 1775-1783, and in 1787 founded the United States.[71]

English Patchwork Styles
circa 1800

In the last years of the Eighteenth Century, small-pattern printed fabrics with flower, leaf, dot and geometric motifs in white and bright colors on dark backgrounds were especially popular for clothing. They characterized the appearance of many patchwork quilts into the Nineteenth Century. Chintzes with big flower, bird, landscape and other pictorial patterns, inspired by the printed textiles from India, were also popular. They usually had white or natural color backgrounds, while from the turn of the century on, red, red-brown and canary yellow were also used. Solid colors and accurate drawn copperplate prints were also produced for many years, but the grayish-yellow colors that had dominated the block prints of the last quarter century disappeared from the palettes of the manufacturers around 1810—and a little later even from the sewing baskets of the patchwork makers.[72]

The Englishwomen sewed patchwork or applique to make daytime bedspreads and covers for the four-poster beds common at the time. These covers, known as coverlets, were unquilted and usually made to fit the shape of the bed. The central pattern took up almost the whole surface of the bed and appeared "hiked up", since only three sides of the coverlet were given a border. Sometimes the corners were also unbordered, so that the cloth could lie flat in spite of the posts that carried the canopy. The fashion of unquilted coverlets endured until about 1830, not the least linked to the strongly patterned textiles that were used. After 1830 solid-color and unpatterned fabrics became more and more popular, and quilting gained popularity along with them.

There were three types of coverlets, each sewn with a different technique and having a different appearance.

Pure applique decoration consisted of a central motif surrounded by bows, ribbons or garlands. These were cut out of colorful printed fabrics. Stars, squares standing on one corner (diamonds), zigzag stripes, and many flower and leaf patterns were appliqued. At the beginning of the century, the textile manufacturers even began to meet the needs of the patchworkers by printing special chintz medallions and borders. These brightly-colored bouquets, baskets of flowers and fruit, garlands and wreaths just needed to be cut out and sewn on. Many quilts of this era are naturally similar because of these same motifs, and show little individuality (#50).

50 Quilt of printed cotton, England, 1805-1820, 279 x 272. Victoria and Albert Museum, London, UK.

51 Patchwork quilt from Wales, early 19th Century, 239 x 211. Victoria and Albert Museum, London, UK.

The combination of applique and patchwork techniques occurs especially often in coverlets around the turn of the century. For the most part, appliqued central motifs were surrounded by patchwork. "Dogtooth" pointed triangles in a row, or "sawtooth" rows of equilateral triangles, were very popular. But all other imaginable combinations of geometric motifs in zigzag or other eye-catching spatial patterns were tried. By means of alternating patterns, rows, dark-light effects and color contrasts, as well as scattered appliques, the basic elements, which were in principle always the same, were varied. The most talented sewing was shown by the patterns in the corners, and it is rewarding to give some attention to the variety of ways in which corners were designed.

Naturally, pure patchwork quilts were also made, and here too medallion-style work prevails. What was said above about forming the corners applies here too, for they were also made up out of geometric elements. The formation of borders developed into striped quilts. They were made of stripes of cloth and bands of patchwork, and had no central motif, but rather what the English called an "all over pattern". The entire surface was covered with one pattern, and individual areas were not stressed. Here the stripes still dominated the pattern, though there are many examples where individual elements, not always the same, were attached to each other, and the complete appearance of the quilt was attained only by the single form and the colors. In the simplest cases this was done with a square or a rectangle.

One of many "typically English" patterns that is found throughout the history of patchwork is the hexagon known as the "honeycomb". It is very simple to make, especially as the individual rosettes allow practically unlimited color variations. Hexagonal work has been known since the late Eighteenth Century. Along with the hexagon, the diamond has also formed the basis of many star and box designs over paper patterns. These give the patchwork stiffness until all the pieces are sewn together. They also keep the geometric angles and edges in line. All of the "all-over patterns" were excellently suited to communal work, and they are found particularly where patchwork was sewn in times of need (#51).

The differences between work done in well-to-do bourgeois households and rural ones can be defined not only by the choice of fabrics. The patterns of country quilts and coverlets are more permanent and traditional, in any case less influenced by whimsical fashions than the quilts of the bourgeois housewives and wealthy classes. One can conclude from this that patchwork and applique were never as popular in England, before or after, than from about 1800 to 1840.[73]

On the other hand, quilting, especially in rural areas, was always done out of real necessity instead of following short-term fashion. Working at home, the country people also made quilts, beyond their own needs, for the great country houses of the aristocracy and wealthy upper bourgeoisie. After their daily work, the mothers, daughters and maids would gather around the quilting frame and work together. Even the youngest were included, in order to learn from their elders. The tradition that a girl had to have twelve quilts in her dowry was widespread in England. The first quilt was relatively simple, but the complexities of the later ones increased with the age and dexterity of the girl. The thirteenth quilt should have been the wedding quilt, and was made only when the girl married. It was the most beautiful and most carefully sewn quilt of all. Hearts were often included in the central motif, and the edge patterns were planned carefully to avoid breaks. It was believed then that a break in the edging at the corners was an omen of unhappiness and a broken marriage. An old rhyme from Devonshire makes a drastic reference to the custom of having quilts in a dowry:

> At your quilting, maids, don't dally,
> Quilt quick if you would marry.
> A maid who is quiltless at twenty-one
> Never shall greet her bridal sun![74]

The emigrants took this custom with them to the New World.

Textile Production in Colonial Days

The English immigrant had separated from his mother country geographically but not culturally when he went to North America. Through strict laws such as the "Navigation Act"[75] that banned trade except with England, the English government tried to nip the colonists' own efforts in the bud. In addition to quilts brought with them by the settlers, a wide variety of new quilts were imported over many years. This shows that there was a great demand. Advertisements for textiles of all kinds, and especially for "bed quilts", were printed in such daily newspapers as the "Boston Newsletter".

W. Eddis, an Englishman who toured the colonies at the end of the Eighteenth Century, stated that he could find few differences between a rich colonist and a rich Briton.[76] This observation makes clear that the imported textiles were affordable mainly in wealthier circles, while many emigrants who were busy building their lives simply could not afford them. They sewed their own quilts, and one can find advertisements in the newspapers for cloth and padding. Even courses teaching the techniques were advertised.[76] But most settlers depended on finding their own raw materials and fabrics, especially when they moved farther west and settled far from the great seaports such as Boston. Along with financial problems, division of markets also played an important role in the choice of materials used in a quilt.

The first settlers found no usable textile fibers in America, and imports could not be the only alternative. Prizes were offered to increase the number of sheep brought from Europe, and ewes could not legally be exported. The situation developed to the point that the inhabitants of Philadelphia swore not to eat lamb any more. But wool still had to be imported for years; as late as 1774, considerable importation of wool to Pennsylvania was reported.

Around 1640 court decisions in Massachusetts and Connecticut decreed that every family had to grow a certain quantity of flax. In addition, at least one member of the family had to work at spinning, which was usually done by children. Three pounds of wool, flax or cotton were to be spun per week, for a fine of twelve pence was levied for every lacking pound.

All of this took place although the English government had banned the ownership of a spinning wheel, the penalty for which was having one's right hand cut off. Textile workers were banned from emigrating to the colonies.[77]

These strict laws, whose purpose was to secure the greatest possible dependence of the American markets on British products, were resisted by the settlers through active cooperation. Despite the mother country's mercantile policies, a modest textile production was able to exist. Many textiles were produced at home through the cooperative work of neighbors.

The English imports included wool, linen and silk fabrics. All the purely cotton textiles from before the Eighteenth Century were made of raw materials or yarn that had to be imported via England from the East Indies. Since the beginning of the Nineteenth Century, all necessary methods of manufacturing cotton textiles industrially were applied in great style in England. The technology of producing printed fabrics was especially important to our subject.

Since 1617 Europe had understood the Oriental technique of etching for coloring and adapted block and copperplate printing to textiles. The invention of the first drum printing machine by the Scotsman Thomas Bell in 1783, in which the color was applied to the cloth by an engraved copper roller, also furthered the development of this process.[78] It allowed the English textile industry to produce high-quality cotton prints at reasonable prices, and these naturally came onto the American market. Eventually textiles were also produced from American raw cotton and then exported back to the colonies. In 1792 George Washington's Secretary of the Treasury, Alexander Hamilton, prepared an inclusive report on the state of various occupations in the colonies. He asserted in it that the cotton industry offered particular advantages to the United States, since the newly invented English machines required workers with only a little training. Through the initiative of Hamilton's close collaborator, Tench Cox, the southern states were encouraged to grow much more cotton, of which little had been cultivated until then. This was exported chiefly to England, for technical development in the colonies had been hindered above all by the English law that banned the exportation of machines for manufacturing cotton, wool, linen and silk. The Americans, lacking experience in technical matters, had only illegal methods of obtaining the necessary knowledge.[79] Until they succeeded at this, they reworked English cloth into textiles for clothing and decoration. The fabrics produced at home served mainly for making household articles. They were simple linen and wool fabrics, or a type known as "linsey-woolsey". This is a very coarse weave of linen or cotton warp and wool weft, which was originally developed in the English town of Suffolk.[80]

Growth of the North American Textile Industry

As long as the settlers were dependent on the mother country, they had few chances to prove their self-sufficiency. This material and cultural dependence is illustrated clearly in the patchwork quilts of colonial days, as the comparison of patchwork and applique techniques shows.

The emigrants from other countries, the French in Canada, the Hollanders in New York, the Swedes and Germans in Pennsylvania, brought their own esthetic standards and production techniques with them. But these replaced the patchwork and applique techniques brought from England only slowly, and also only in certain regions. Independence from England and the development of the American textile industry created new requirements, even for the existence of patchwork quilts.

Since the last decade of the Eighteenth Century, cotton had been grown extensively in the southern states. Since 1795 little was grown besides cotton in the plantation area of the South, save for the simplest foodstuffs for the slaves. The textile-producing sites of the time, with their simple machines, lacked the industrial technology to handle the great quantities of available raw material. The greatest problem was that the cotton had to have its seeds removed before it could be processed in any known way. Until the invention of the "cotton gin", the deseeding machine, by Eli Whitney in 1793, this had to be done by hand. One person took about two years to deseed a bale of cotton; the new machine rid fifteen bales of their clinging seeds in one day. One can imagine that this invention created completely new potentialities almost overnight, thereby making the United States one of the great cotton producers.

The disparity between the speeds of the spinning and weaving processes was also especially glaring. Attempts were made to bring to America the spinning machine developed by Richard Arkwright in 1769. But success was gained only by the textile worker Samuel Slater, who embarked in disguise in 1789 and emigrated to America with the plans for the machine in his head. A small textile firm in Providence, Rhode Island, contracted to build the machine. This led in 1793 to the start of production by the first North American cotton spinning mill of Almy, Brown and Slater, in Pawtucket, Rhode Island, using three carding and two spinning machines driven by an old mill. Only the weaving was still done on looms in the neighborhood, though the bleaching, dyeing and finishing of the thread could also be done in the mill. Slater insisted, though, on using West Indian cotton, because it was supposedly of better quality than the American.

In 1794, presumably at the urging of his wife Hannah Wilkinson, he produced the first cotton sewing thread. Until then linen, silk and wool thread had been common, since hand-spun cotton thread was weak. This new cotton thread was triple-strand, and after 1840, six-strand thread was also produced and used in sewing.[81]

Samuel Slater founded several other spinning mills and a wool-weaving mill. These mills became the centers around which the cities of Webster and Manchester, New Hampshire, were built. He gave the impetus to the development of the cotton industry in the United States, where in 1807 there were only 8000 spindles, but by 1825 already 800,000.

A further improvement was the introduction of the mechanical loom. In 1812 the first cotton-weaving mill was established in Lowell, Massachusetts, and in 1823 it spawned the first calico factory, soon followed by many others. For practical reasons, the weaving mills were usually built near the existing spinning mills. By 1825 the North American cotton industry, with its center in New England, was developed in all its essential components.[82]

Unlike the weaving mills, the dyeing industry developed slowly. For a long time, textiles were dyed almost exclusively at home, though this work was complicated and demanding. The formulas for the dyestuffs were naturally used and handed on like recipes for cakes. Their basic ingredients grew in forests and gardens: oak and maple for violet and purple, scarlet berries for grayish-blue, walnut bark and husks for brown, sumac berries for dark red, hickory or red oak bark for brown and yellow shades, indigo for blue, madder, cochineal and logwood for red and blue shades, and many, many more.

During the century, the technology of dyeing and printing textiles was further developed and put to industrial use in North America following European examples.[83]

Patchwork and Quilts
in the Colonies after 1750

The North American quilts of colonial days can easily be described before this background. Wool, cotton, linen, silk and mixed weaves such as linsey-woolsey were available for quilting. But a special favorite was a pure wool worsted cloth called "Calamanco", imported from England and France since the middle of the Eighteenth Century. It was used above all to make bed curtains, upholstered furniture and also clothing. This light wool fabric had a glossy (chintzlike) or moirelike surface, produced after weaving through pressure or heating and the use of a special solution. Patterns similar to damask could also be applied with pressure or heat. Calamanco was dyed in clear, handsome colors and was excellent material with which to make quilts (#54). These were known as linsey-woolsey quilts, even when they were covered with linsey-woolsey only on the back.[84] They were regarded as the most elegant quilts at that time. As "wholecloth quilts" they remained in solid colors and were made more artistic only with quilting patterns whose forms were borrowed from nature. A screen of diagonal lines crossing each other formed a background from which flowers, pineapples, palm leaves, grapes, tendrils and feathers rose up as in relief. Very thin quilting was necessart as long as raw cotton or carded wool was used for the interlining. It was not only especially decorative, but also prevented the sliding and clumping of the filling.

The showpieces among the pure quilts were the "white work" quilts,[85] that were made very lovingly of white linen or cotton. Their greatest era extended from the last quarter of the Eighteenth Century to the middle of the Nineteenth, when applique quilts gained increasingly great popularity. Even today, though, they are still made in traditional form by devoted quilters.

Just as quilting continued to follow the principles of the medallion style, as was still common in England, this can also be said of the patchwork of that time. But the close link with England can be documented not only in stylistic terms, but also in the materials used. One difference may be that in America we usually find patchwork quilts that have a very practical value along with their decorative worth. In England the unquilted "coverlets" were regarded as particularly fine, and have been preserved in greater numbers even to

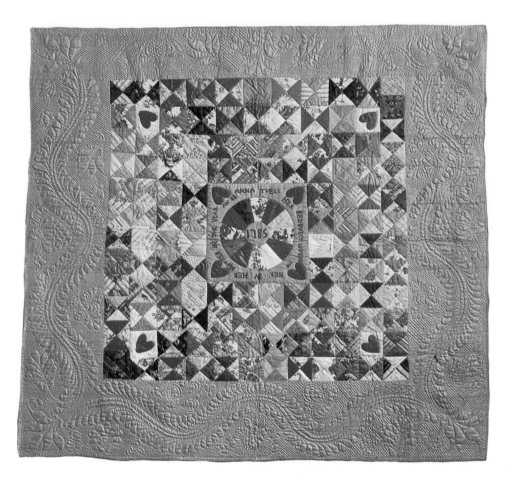

52 Anna Tuels' wedding quilt, Maine, 1785, 218x206. Wadsworth Atheneum, Hartford, Connecticut, USA. (see also protective coverings)

this day, although there were patchwork quilts at the same time. The difference is surely based on the fact that in England it was mainly the ladies of the middle classes, the upper bourgeoisie who occupied themselves with patchwork, applique and quilting. In America every quilt speaks of necessity, no matter how beautifully it is designed in color, form and pattern.

From the times before 1750,[86] as far as we know, no North American patchwork quilt has survived until today. The oldest example[87] is Anna Tuels' wedding quilt (#52). Since it includes the inscription: "Anna Tuels her quilt given to her by her mother in the year Au 23 1785«, it can be dated easily. A patchwork pattern made solely of triangles is arranged around a central square with a circle divided into segments. Around it is a wide pink border made of wool cloth and quilted with large leaves and vines. Eight appliqued hearts mark this quilt as a wedding quilt, as was customary in many areas.

53 Harlequin calamanco quilt from New England, 1800-1820, 223 x 221. Historic Deerfield, Inc., Deerfield, Massachusetts, USA.

Two other quilts from the last years of the Eighteenth Century indicate the clear relationship to English work. The quilt of Mary Johnston, made in 1793 (#55), and the quilt ascribed to Martha Washington show centers of chintz with designs applied by copper-plate printing. They are trimmed with borders of appliqued flowers in the style known as "broderie perse" and with triangles in "Wild

54 Glazed indigo wool quilt, sewn by Esther Wheat of Conway, Massachusetts, early 19th Century, 236 x 231. Smithsonian Institution, Washington, D.C, USA.

Goose Chase'' and windmill patterns.[88] The combination of domestic weaves and imported fabrics generally give the impression that hand-woven cloth was, whenever possible, limited to the back, while English printed textiles were preferred for the appliques and patchwork patterns of the front.

Along with these English-looking quilts, a somewhat more individual treatment of the medallion style was already developing (#53). The formation of linsey-woolsey quilts with large areas of two or three colors went one step farther, keeping the principle of the central motif but changing in terms of larger-surface color and shape composition. This is definitive of the first impression of the decoration—the quilting fascinates the eye at the second look. Being limited to the simplest geometric basic forms reduced the medallion pattern to its essential characteristics and makes these quilts the first representatives of a more and more typical and uniquely developed North American quilt tradition.

In addition, there were quilts sewn together of squares, the fields being decorated with varying quilt patterns. This forerunner of the "block style" that developed later corresponds in its construction to the checkered woven blankets of the time, every square of which was ornamented with wool embroidery.[89] The designs give the impression of a collection of patterns rather than rows of the same motifs.

Unfortunately, only a few examples of these quilts from the latter half of the Eighteenth Century have survived. Most of them were worn out by long use and frequent washing, and had seen their best days as clothing before they were finally made into quilts. So this, like the turkey soup made of the leftover scraps of the Christmas roast, was a last positive appearance.[90]

55 Patchwork and appliqué quilt by Mary Johnston, North Carolina, 1793, 246 x 203. Henry Francis du Pont, Winterthur Museum, Winterthur, Delaware, USA.

Aspects of 19th-Century
North American History

It seems interesting to ask the question of what the historical background was from which American folk art of the Nineteenth Century developed. One could do without a look behind the scenes if it were not so helpful in understanding these objects, and especially quilts. Everywhere one encounters indications that, on the one hand, are relevant only to ordinary everyday life, yet hint, on the other hand, at political and religious relationships that are not familiar to us. A rough sketch of the great American themes of those times can at least begin to give us explanations and inspire us to go deeper into the matter.

This beginning is not so roundabout, for in 1949 Marguerite Ickis sought to make a historical division of American quilt production into five clearly differentiated periods. The first was the "Colonial Period", in which the products looked almost exactly like those of the countries from which the quilters emigrated. Next came the "Revolutionary Era" with its French accents, strawflowers cut out of toile and applied to a background. Then came the "Pioneer Period", the era when the west was won, ending with the Gold Rush of the Forty-niners. The "Civil War Era" of the Fifties and Sixties preceded the "Centennial Period". Since the early 1880»s the art of quilting, except in isolated villages and farms in the Midwest and mountain cabins in the Great Smokies, has been dealt its deathblow by steam-driven machines and industrially produced needlework.[91]

It obviously could not have been that simple, for even the quilts of the Colonial and Revolutionary eras are much more different in their appearance than this strict scheme would allow. The history should rather be seen as a fertile soil in which the culture, including that of handicrafts, could grow within flexible boundaries.

The people who founded and built up America's independence since 1776 were very interested in maintaining it too. They went about their work optimistically and energetically, helping themselves in areas where the state had no authority or influence. No political topic was too insignificant for them to look into. The greatest challenge of the Nineteenth Century was to settle and organize the western part of the continent. Even before 1800 the Appalachians had been crossed and people were moving westward in covered wagons, to settle down in some suitable place as farmers, merchants or craftsmen. This movement essentially proceeded as a socioeconomic expansion, without wars other than those against England (1812-1814) and Mexico (1845-1848) and the frequent and bloody fighting with the Indians. A particular impetus for the opening of the West was the massive flow of immigrants from England, Ireland, Germany and Scandinavia around 1830.

During the first quarter of the century the Democrats, who relied above all on the farmers and poorer levels of the population for their support, were dominant politically. The vastness of the country and the constant movement of many inhabitants made political influence difficult. But the people's awareness of their involvement in building a country made them receptive to political subjects, though often in a very self-willed way. When the western agricultural states finally made their political wishes known, this led in 1828 to a division into two parties, the Democrats and the Whigs (Liberals, and later Republicans). The differences between the northern and southern states, supported as they were by different economic systems, also became explosive when it at last focused on the issue of slavery. The southern states circumvented the ban of slave importation, while in the North there was increased involvement in the anti-slavery movement. As long as most of the powerful politicians came from the South, the problem could not be solved. But the economic advantages of the free states through the fast development of industry, trade and banking made itself felt more and more in terms of political strength in comparison to the economy of the South, based only on the growing of cotton.

Around the middle of the century, the dispute about slavery flared up with all its might. It led to the secession of ten states from the union in 1861 and their forming a confederation. In the Civil War of 1861-1865, much of which took place in Virginia, the political disagreements escalated into open warfare. The surrender of the Confederate States in 1865 finally set the slaves free, which was then established in the Constitution. As United States citizens, the blacks received the right to vote in 1868 (women only in 1920). The last southern states were readmitted to the union in 1870, and the last federal troops withdrawn in 1877.

Just after the war, the first transcontinental railway was completed, and by 1890 the opening of the West was substantially complete. Industrialization, progress in economy and technology were pushed onward in grand style and highly praised. The old middle classes of independent farmers and small businessmen were replaced by a class whose jobs were created by industry: employees, skilled workers, technicians and managers. The economic prospects lured many emigrants to America again around the turn of the century.[92]

The historical conditions explain the political perplexity of any individual. The rate of change was such that it even found expression in folk arts. And the fact that these reflected a close link to nature as well as a sense of community and religious faith can be explained by the historical events. The separation of state and church existed since the founding of the United States, so that the wide variety of religious denominations worked diligently to attract members. But the conditions make it seem logical that religious faith was for many people like an anchor in those stormy times, supplying unity and security.

Much of that which has been described above fell to earth in the patchwork quilts of the Nineteenth Century. Now it needs to be recognized and elucidated.

Social Significance of Quilts in North America

There are vivid reports of life in North America during the first half of the Nineteenth Century. To the outsider it seems to have been a very hard life, including all the difficulties of a new beginning. Dramatic stories tell of lives filled with poverty and privation, especially for those who headed westward from the East Coast to open up new lands and new opportunities for themselves. In the process, the patchwork quilts of the English, Scottish and Irish immigrants who settled deeper and deeper in the Appalachian hill country reached its highest development.[93]

56 Rocinda Winslow, Wilson Quilt, North Carolina, 1830-1840. The Mint Museum, Charlotte, North Carolina, USA.

Only the intensive discussion with the social and historical conditions of the New World shows that the conditions must be regarded in very differentiated ways when one looks for aspects that are to illuminate the history of the patchwork quilt.

Before the American Revolution, for example, Irish of Scottish descent, Ulstermen, moved out of Pennsylvania and Maryland into the area around Charlotte, North Carolina at the foot of the Appalachians, near its southern boundary with South Carolina. They emigrated originally for religious reasons, since they stood, as Presbyterians, for their religion and religious freedom and were especially in favor of the separation of church and state. Their area was Mecklenburg County, and they settled there on large plantations which were worked with the help of slaves. They were the first to declare themselves independent of England in 1775, and they took part in the Revolution as particularly willing and zealous volunteers. The inhabitants of Mecklenburg County were essentially cultivated, prosperous and hospitable people. They lived by growing cotton, and after the war also profited from the production of many notable gold mines.

Their parties were very popular, and often included a gathering of the women for quilting. Quilting went on in the community until darkness set in, and then a festive dinner and dance took place. The guests, some of whom had ridden in from distant plantations, stayed overnight and required great numbers of guest rooms, beds and quilts. Many medallion quilts, especially beautiful by the standards set by English models, have survived from these days (#56). But it was not just the English models, on which the Ulstermen must rather have had mixed feelings, that explains the special preference for these quilts. They are worked above all in the "broderie perse" manner. Patterns were cut out of imported chintzes and applied to a white background. These chintzes were expensive, and if one could use such great numbers of them, that was a sign of the wealth that prevailed in the house.

The significance of just such quilts, which were also made communally for parties or weddings, is clear: they were status symbols and expressions of social recognition (#58).

A letter from Marry Warren of the Davidson Plantation to Mary Springs in 1800 reflects the value of quilts in this society very nicely: "I am so busy amusing myself here, as there is nothing else for us here but quiltings and weddings . . .".[94] Quilting was thus synonymous with celebrating, and patterns which displayed wealth and worldliness were correspondingly popular. So much value was placed on quilts that they were listed in last wills along with slaves, furniture, silver, household linens, money and land.[94]

*57 "The Quilting Party", circa 1870. Abby Aldrich Rockefeller Folk Art Center,
Williamsburg, Virginia, USA.*

Characteristic of the life-style and attitude of the people, especially
those in New England, during the first half of the Nineteenth
Century, is the following quotation from the foreword of a book, very
popular in its day, about housekeeping, Lydia Maria Child's "The
American Frugal Housewife", the 31st edition of which came out in
1845:

> "The real economy of a household is shown in the art of
> gathering all leftovers, so that nothing is wasted. I mean
> leftovers of time as well as material. Nothing should be
> thrown away as long as the possibility remains of putting it to
> use, as meager as it may be; and however large the family may
> be, every member of it should keep busy earning his money or
> saving money . . . In reference to this, patchwork is a good
> means of saving. It is naturally a crazy waste of time to tear
> cloth to pieces in order to arrange it anew into fantastic
> patterns; but a large family may be maintained on
> insignificant things and a few shillings may be saved through
> the use of curtain and clothing scraps,"[95]

58 Charlotte Dabney, applique quilt, Dorchester, Maryland, circa 1799, 250 x 233. Cincinnati Art Museum, Cincinnati, Ohio, USA.

The quilts referred to here naturally looked different from the applique quilts from Mecklenburg County, North Carolina. They were simple patchwork quilts (#59, 60, 61). This advice speaks for the revolutionary ideals of the time, in which work was seen as the basis of family life and family life as the foundation of every community. In this respect, patchwork quilts were regarded as a product of community effort.

The so-called "quiltings" were gatherings with an important function within the social life of rural and urban communities. Helping each other mutually was taken for granted in those days by townspeople and farmers. They gathered for all imaginable occasions to help each other, whether in building a barn or cleaning and carding wool.

The word "bee", so often used in connection with quilts, and borrowed from busy bees to mean a meeting of industrious women sewing a quilt, was actually never used. Letters and diaries of the time use only the expression "quilting"; the "quilting bees" were invented afterward by romanticizing authors.

In a letter written by Friederike Bremer in 1849, the meaning of the word "bee" is explained:

"I was at a 'bee'! And if you'd like to know what this creation of society here is, pay attention! When a family falls into poverty through illness or fire and the children need clothing and other things, some of the better-off ladies in the neighborhood get together at once and sew for them. Such a gathering is called a 'bee'!" [96]

59 Stripe quilt, "S. G. 1871", made of European cotton chintzes, 254 x 236. American Museum in Britain, Claverton Manor, Bath, UK.

60 Sarah Corwyn quilt, New England, 1831, with detail, 272 x 240. Privately owned by Ute Bredow, Berlin, West Germany.

Detail of #60.

94

61 Ruth Poeter's quilt, 1777?, 244 x 231. American Museum in Britain, Claverton Manor, Bath, UK.

In addition, there were many other bees that served to complete necessary or less pleasant tasks in the community.

In comparison to these, quiltings were an all-around enjoyable occasion at which people could get together and talk while working creatively (#57). Here was an opportunity to show a knowledgeable public one's latest creation, exchange new ideas for patchwork and quilt patterns, sew a communal quilt for someone who was to be particularly honored, make a bridal quilt, which amounted to an engagement announcement in many regions, and finally to share all the news of the nearer and farther sourounding area. It is obvious that a capable seamstress had a good social position in such circumstances—the inept were sent to the kitchen. So it was desirable for even a little girl to become a good seamstress. Quiltings were events that included all levels of society or, better put, all those who were interested in an active social life.

Development of the Patchwork Block Pattern

The formation of patchwork quilts was based above all on sewing together pieces of worn-out clothing or draperies. It is easy to imagine that suitable pieces of cloth were exchanged in the neighborhood in order to solve certain problems of matching colors. In spite of all its practical aspects, patchwork offered the opportunity to work creatively with colors and shapes. In any other context, such activity would be criticized as a waste of time, which one was simply not allowed to do under the prevailing conditions. But since the result was the production of very useful and decorative quilts, patchwork was tolerated and made into a social occasion by the holding of quiltings.

To be sure, we must first put the significance of patchwork into perspective by making clear in what situation a woman normally found herself around the turn of the century. For example, all the household and family textile production was her responsibility. That means that all textiles had to be produced, from raw materials to finished clothing or draperies. The help of neighbors and servants, depending on her social position, made this task easier. But in view of these conditions, it is understandable why even four-year-old girls were put to work at sewing. With the growing industrialization of textile production, women were relieved of a lot of work, but the time that remained for patchwork and quilting is still not ample to measure. It was a "spare-time activity" for evening hours, as long as no socks needed to be darned or work clothes patched. It is hard to imagine that, as it appears, the poorer women should have done so much patchwork. Could they really spare the time and energy when they had to prepare at least the necessities for the family? There is much to suggest that this activity required a rather healthy economic situation in the family. Too-romanticized historical writings have perhaps glossed over this fact too much.

The early patchwork quilts that have survived since 1750 were for the most part made of linsey-woolsey and sewn of large-section geometric pieces of cloth. Formed in two or three colors, they reduced the medallion style to its basic elements. Very few examples of linsey-woolsey quilts show more intricate patterns, but even these combine only two or three colors in patterns of squares, stripes or triangles. In a way, these point to the *block patterns* that were used more and more since the beginning of the Nineteenth Century. These were made of basic squares in a handy size, which were divided in a wide variety of ways to form new patterns and could be sewn together as desired. The simplest form, the *one patch* or undivided square, produced deliberate color compositions, checkerboard patterns, or in rectangle form made "brickwall" patterns also known as hit and miss. Divided into four equally large squares, the equilateral rectangle became the basis of the *four patch*. Diagonal lines could divide them again, so as to develop many *diamond* and *triangle* patterns.

A square divided into nine smaller squares could be divided in still different ways, forming the basis of countless star patterns that were particularly popular (#62). This *nine patch* was followed by the "sixteen patch" pattern and so on.

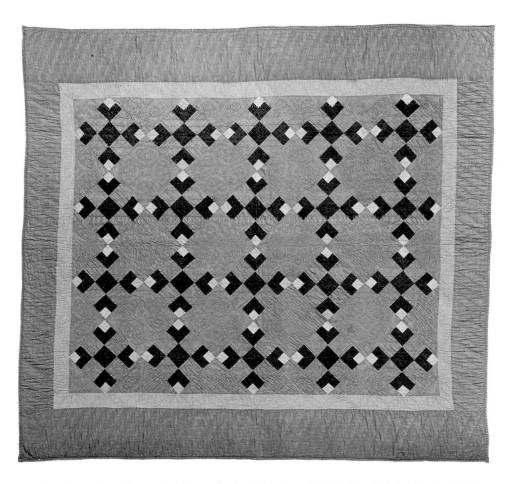

62 Patchwork quilt, "Nine Patch", Amish, circa 1920, 174 x 157. Folk Art Gallery, Hamburg, West Germany.

63 Various block patterns, Folk Art Gallery, Hamburg, West Germany:
a "Grandmother's Flower Garden" (hexagonal);
b "Diamond";
c Applique block;
d Log Cabin variation.

98

64 Various block patterns, Folk Art Gallery, Hamburg, West Germany;
a Sixteen Patch;
b "Goose Tracks" or "Cross and Crown";
c "Le Moyne Star";
d "Melon Patch" combined with "Nine Patch" block.

The principle consisted by arranging the individual squares with diagonal lines. The elements of the block that originated thereby were accented in color in various ways, so as to obtain a certain pattern. The blocks sewn together produced rows of the same pattern or combined into an "all over" design in which an individual block was noticed only at second glance. Combining pattern blocks with solid-color ones was just as common as combining stripes in contrasting colors, forming a grid between the blocks.

The method before the block system built a patchwork by repeating even the same geometric elements. Hexagons or diamonds formed patterns, usually developing from the center out, that were made only by colors, not by combining differently shaped components. It was called the 'English method" when all the parts that made up such a design were attached to paper patterns before being sewn. As the name suggests, this technique was widespread in England during the Nineteenth and Twentieth Centuries. But in America too it continued to exist along with the block pattern, especially as one of the greatest and best-loved patchwork motifs, the "Le Moyne Star", was made solely out of diamond shapes.

On the other hand, sewing blocks was much more practical. Handy squares were made of the individual elements, these were combined into stripes, and finally all was sewn together into a whole. With the development of the patchwork block method, which made possible an unbelievable array of different patchwork patterns, the North American women created a typical characteristic of their quilts (#63, 64). In the quilts made before 1800, the central motif still prevailed. After the turn of the century, patchwork quilts made in block style became more and more popular. Most surviving quilts made before 1825 came from New York, Pennsylvania and Maryland, a few from Virginia, the New England states and elsewhere. All the basic block patterns already exist in them, especially the simpler ones such as *Diamond in the Square, Variable Star* and other star blocks. *Sawtooth* variations were also widespread, either as border patterns or as blocks for *Delectable Mountains* and *Birds in the Air,* as well as the most varied "Nine Patch" blocks.[97] The block patterns bore names that developed from a combination of their original history and surroundings and can be explained today only conditionally. The older a pattern is, the more it has been in circulation and the more names it bears.[98]

Patterns and Motifs:
Names and Meanings

Most of the patterns that are still in use today already existed at the begining of the Nineteenth Century. They were handed on from mother to daughter, taken along in covered wagons to be shown to new friends, sold at country fairs or acquired from traveling peddlers. The names of these patterns mirror hard times, the beauty of nature, religious dedication and political trends. Patriotism and pioneer spirit became part of American folk art in them. A pattern sometimes changed not only its colors, but even its name in its travels.[99]

It is impossible to introduce all patterns and their many variations and names here. There are lexicons and institutions that have made this their task.[100] The impetus and background that gave birth to a

65 Patchwork quilt, "Goose in the Pond". Folk Art Gallery, Hamburg.

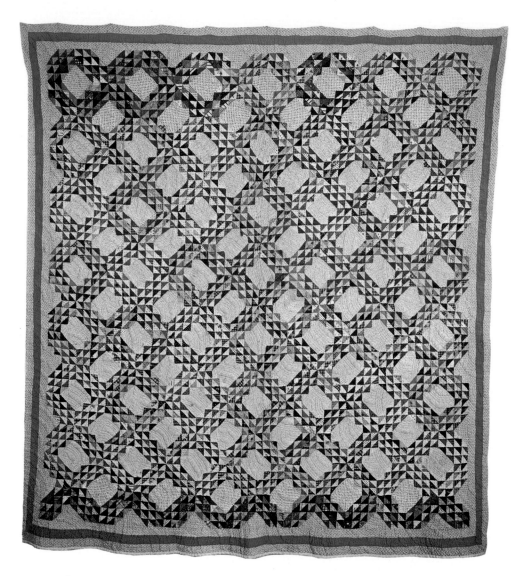

66 Patchwork quilt, "Ocean Waves", 206 x 182. Folk Art Gallery, Hamburg..

pattern or its name are many. Appliqued patterns usually have their origins in the world of nature. Flowers, leaves, rare animals and people were their sources. For the patchwork patterns, which tend somewhat toward the abstract as a result of their formative technique, the sources of inspiration are often much less concrete.

At first there was the possibility of adapting real objects, flowers, houses, trees and fences, into geometric basic forms so as still to be recognizable as the object in question. Here the general characterization was still sufficient to portray concrete patterns. "Schoolhouse" or "Basket" blocks are examples that illustrate this principle.

More general pictures from nature, such as the flight of wild geese, ocean waves or bear tracks were visible phenomena that could be reproduced abstractly (#66). Their adaptation into geometric form suggested the impression of flying geese, rolling waves and bear tracks but could also be interpreted in other ways. So small triangles usually became the symbol for birds, not only for smaller types but for geese, ducks and chickens too (#65). A combination of large and small triangles can, under certain conditions, represent a hen with chicks. How fanciful the interpretations and thus the names could be is seen clearly in the old "Bear's Paw"[102] pattern (#67). In its name it reflects the dangers that came with living on the edge of the Wild West and in proximity to wild bears. In more populated areas, where bears were on the decline but back roads, streets and paths were still muddy, the pattern was called "Duck's Foot in the Mud". The Quakers of Philadelphia were very differently inspired by it and named it "Hands of Friendship". This happened to many patterns on their way across the United States, and the reasons for the names are often even more fanciful than the patterns themselves.

67 Patchwork quilt, "Bear's Paw", circa 1880, 215 x 212. Atef-Schreiterer Collection, Berlin, West Germany.

103

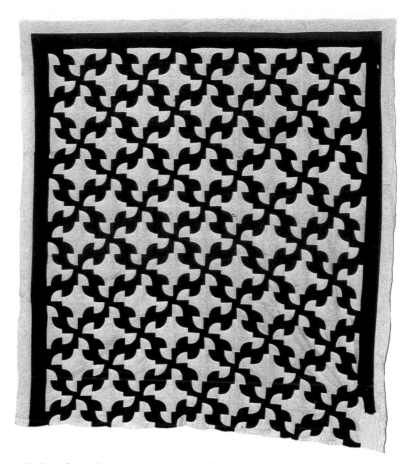

68 Patchwork Top, "Drunkard's Path", 230 x 200. Privately owned by Rosa Dames, Berlin, West Germany.

A further abstraction is shown in the geometric patterns that illustrate only ideas and conceptions, such as the path of a drunkard, a hole in the barn or a trip around the world (#68). Here the question arises of whether the pattern inspired the name or the name led to the pattern. They are still readable when one knows their names, but the names too were changeable. The abstract pattern made many associations possible. Thus the "Drunkard's Path", even before 1845, was called the "Rocky Road to Dublin", "Rocky Road to California" or "Country Husband". In Ohio the pattern got the name of "Robbing Peter to Pay Paul".[102] In any case, it was a very popular, simple pattern with a vivid effect.

The biggest group of patchwork patterns were those that were fully abstract and hinted at an idea or event. The existence of countless "Rocky Roads to . . ." originated—as already suggested-in long,

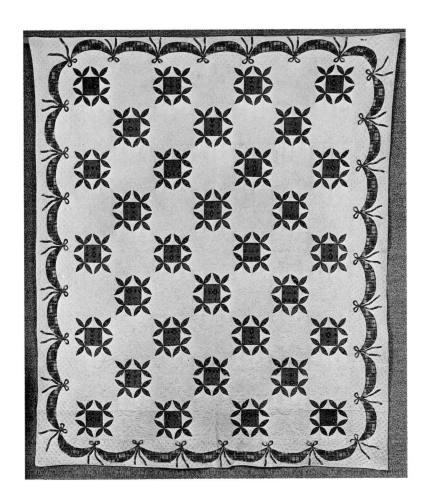

69 "Wandering Foot" or "Turkey Track" quilt, Maryland, 1840-
50, 239 x 203. American Museum in Britain, Claverton Manor,
Bath, UK.

bone-shaking travels westward in covered wagons. The inspirations
for the naming of these patterns are scarcely conceivable for today's
observer. Events of a very personal kind, within a family or
neighborhood, have played just as great a role as political, religious
or literary references. Sometimes a certain superstition was embodied
in the symbolism of a pattern or its name. A few examples can
illustrate this statement very well.[103]

A little history is recounted in the naming of the "Lafayette Orange
Peel" pattern. During a banquet in Philadelphia in honor of the
Marquis de Lafayette, Spanish oranges were served. These rare fruits
aroused much attention, and a young lady took an orange home with
her. She peeled the fruit carefully and developed from it a patchwork
pattern that bears this impressive name to this day.[104]

70 Patchwork quilt, "Jacob's Ladder", Iowa Amish, circa 1920, 218 x 178. Verena Klüser Quilt Gallery, Munich, West Germany.

71 Patchwork quilt, "Delectable Mountains", Iowa Amish, circa 1920, 217 x 160. Verena Klüser Quilt Gallery, Munich, West Germany.

72 "Tulip Quilt", circa 1920, 216 x 212. Folk Art Gallery, Hamburg, West Germany.

Belief and religion were a vital part of life, and thus many patchwork patterns had names with religious associations. The motif that had borne the name "Job's Tears" since 1800 was renamed "Slave Chain" in 1825, thereby giving a hint as to the spirit of the times before the Civil War, when slavery was a more burning issue than religion. In 1840, when Texas had declared its independence from Mexico and applied for admission to the union as the 28th state, the pattern received a new name, "Texas Tears". After the Civil War it was also called "Rocky Road to Kansas', "Kansas Troubles", and finally it was called "Endless Chain".[105]

The "Jacob's Ladder" pattern was so called in New England, while being called "Stepping Stones" in Virginia, "Tail of Benjamin's Kite" in Pennsylvania, "Wagon Tracks" in Mississippi and "Underground Railroad" in Kentucky. The last name takes up the reference to slavery again, for by "Underground Railroad" was meant nothing else than the secret paths of escape for slaves, which stretched from Missouri to Kansas, Nebraska and Iowa.[106] and finally to Canada.

"The Delectable Mountains" is a pattern with whose name the women expressed their love of the land by a reference to to John Bunyan's "Pilgrim's Progress" (#71). There the "Delectable Mountains" are the place from which one can see the Garden of Eden.[107]

Superstition was for a long time the fate of a pattern called "Wandering Foot" (#69). As a matter of principle, one never allowed children to sleep under a quilt with this pattern, for it was believed they would then grow up to be unhappy and restless. No bride wanted to have such a quilt in her hope chest.[108] But the curse was broken by renaming it "Turkey Tracks", otherwise it probably would have died out. When done in green cloth on a white background, it was called "Iris Leaf".

The renaming of the "Hickory Leaf" pattern to "Order No. 11" had a political and also very personal reason. As a ten-year-old girl, Fannie Krieger Hall had to watch while plunderers ripped her mother's new quilt from the bed and took it with them. Order No. 11 established martial law, and when she used the same pattern in a quilt of her own making many years later, she named it "Order No. 11« as a reminder of the injustice that her family had undergone before martial law.[109]

The many variations of the "North Carolina Lily", "Mountain Lily" and such, come from a time of opulent life on the great plantations of the southern states, when there was still enough time to invent and sew such complicated patterns (#72). The lily and tulip patterns are very similar. The lily was usually smaller and more delicate in color and shape, while the tulips were bigger and more colorful. They generally served as symbols of fruitfulness.

Roses were themselves a very straightforward motif, but the liberal politicians' "Whig Rose", the "Democrat Rose", "Harrison Rose" and "Mexican Rose" were all very similar, and there even flared up a disagreement as to which political camp the rose had originally belonged to. The Whigs claimed it just as the Democrats did, and no agreement was possible.[110] The "Radical Rose", with its black center around which the flower petals were arranged, originated during the Civil War to symbolize the freeing of the slaves.[112]

The rose motif is found noticeably in quilts with patriotic themes, sewn to honor a political figure or event. Their political symbolism seems to run unbroken to this day, as the United States Senate had a serious discussion in 1985 on the question of whether the rose or the marigold should be declared the American National Flower.[113] The designing of quilts from the time of the Civil War could offer an answer to this question.

Quilt Patterns in Patchwork Quilts

The simplest quilts, also called "comforters", were made exclusively of the remains of old clothes. Their fronts were assembled of geometrical forms, mostly rectangles and squares. Carded wool, rags or cut-up quilts served as interlining. The three layers were tacked or tied at regular intervals, for which reason these covers were also known as "tack-quilts". Meant to be purely utilitarian, they could be made quickly, even though they had only short lives (#73). During the pioneer days before the Civil War they were very widespread, at least west of the Appalachians. Later they were seen only in poorer rural areas.[113]

Any patchwork quilt, no matter how simple, was superior to these "tack-quilts" in decoration and durability which resulted from the quilting. Normally the various geometric and colorful patchwork patterns were sewn with seams that formed a grid of diagonal, intersecting or parallel lines (#74a-f). A kind of clamshell pattern of opposed arcs was also used, as was a coffee-cup (or, in England, wine-glass) pattern of intersecting circles. A meander pattern of tiny stitches covering the surface evenly in unplanned small, tight curves, offered the possibility, as did the other variations, of quilting a patchwork so that its effect in color and form was not affected. The purely functional purpose of binding the three layers of cloth together and making the quilt sturdier is dominant in this work.

73 Tack-quilt of triangles, circa 1920, 200 x 165. Atef-Schreiterer Collection, Berlin, West Germany.

Naturally, fine quilting was only possible when suitable inter-lining was available. A thick wool lining could only be tacked or tied. A thin lining of raw cotton created the best conditions for stitching, and now and then thin carded wool was also used. Before the colonies gained their independence, most interlinings were imported from England, as is documented by many written sources.[114] But the homemade cotton linings soon prevailed. Since raw cotton had to be cleaned manually until the invention of the cotton gin in 1790 and its widespread use, most quilts up to then contain an interlining with a large proportion of seed pods and foreign bodies. Only in the southern states, where slaves did the difficult job of cleaning the cotton, do we find pure, costly cotton interlinings at an early date. Theories have been made in hopes of finding a basis in this development for the dating of old quilts.[115] But since handmade raw cotton interlinings have been made to this day, especially in rural areas, the points of reference are scarcely usable. The quilting stitches had to be made very small and even to hold the cotton in place and prevent displacement or clumping when washed. The especially fine handwork that we admire so much in old quilts again has a very practical background.

The quilting could emphasize the patchwork pattern to a greater or lesser degree. The simplest means of emphasis was to extend the sewing angles of the individual patchwork elements into parallel quilting seams. In this way it was not necessary to draw in the quilting pattern in advance, and in addition, the sometimes difficult sewing of quilting seams over patchwork seams was avoided. The patchwork, which otherwise would have looked fairly flat, now took on a new dimension.

A further development and heightening of effect was achieved by extending the patchwork lines as quilting onto the neutral borders of the quilt or over solid-color blocks within the quilt. Patchwork and quilt thus became dominated by the same geometry. This made them resemble each other and at the same time produced a mutually effective heightening.

Along with the use of purely geometric patterns, their combination with ornamental quilt motifs was also very popular (#74c, d). On neutral blocks, inlaid stripes or other free surfaces there was enough room for decorative quilting patterns. The contrasting of geometric patterns with ornamental motifs corresponds to the formative principle of wholecloth quilts, which also included a mutual heightening. The quilt motifs, such as flowers, leaves, birds, garlands, wreaths, feathers and many others, corresponded to those of the pure quilts (#74e, f). They were transferred onto the cloth with the help of patterns. Plates, cups, mugs, glasses and coins could be used as well as patterns made of paper, wood, copper and other materials with the designs drawn on them in advance. They were traced around with chalk, a pencil or a pointed pin and so transferred their shape to the cloth. Then one quilted along these lines, and what did not disappear during this work was removed at the first washing.

Quilting played an outstanding role in applique quilts, more and more of which were done in block patterns after the second quarter of the Nineteenth Century. These quilts had replaced the medallion quilts or the pure white wholecloth quilts in the role of showpieces. The motifs, usually applied to white backgrounds, were enhanced by

a

c

b

d

74 Quilting patterns.
Folk Art Gallery, Hamburg, West Germany.
a) Quilting lines over patchwork.
b) Quilting grid over applique.
c) Quilted wreath of feathers on a free one-color block.
d) Quilting motif of an Amish quilt.
e) Quilted leaves and vines in a patchwork border.
f) Quilted garland of feathers on a wide one-color border.

quilting so that, for example, an appliqued bouquet of flowers was completed by adding quilted leaves. Another possibility was that of repeating the whole appliqued motif in a solid-color block, in the center of the quilt or on the border, as a quilting motif. In the end, these variations became just as varied as the quilts themselves that have survived from the Nineteenth Century.[116]

The method of quilting tells us a great deal about the value and place of patchwork and applique quilts at the time of their origin. The particularly artistic quilts surely had an outstanding significance for the women who sewed them. They were well cared for, in some

e

f

cases used only for festive occasions, and seldom if ever washed. Like family jewels, they were passed on from generation to generation, often accompanied by stories of their place in the family's history. Patchwork quilts with simple quilting were meant more for daily use. Often enough their preservation was due to chance, and then it can usually be seen that they were used. They are much more rarely signed than the artistically quilted patchwork and applique quilts, since neither the patchwork nor the applique pattern had been designed with any great outlay of time and trouble. Very, very seldom are the aforementioned "tack-quilts" found, though these surely were made in the greatest numbers. So the more valuable works that have survived may well give us a false picture of the production and use of patchwork quilts in the Nineteenth Century. Only with the rising bourgeois class, a certain economic security and the phenomenon of free time were great numbers of time-consuming patchwork and applique quilts made. This "march of time" can be seen very well in the quilts, and it culminates in the fashion of the "crazy quilt".

The work was done by the group at the quilting, where in one day several utilitarian quilts could be finished. But quilting was also done alone or in the family, especially in winter. The quilt was spread out on a quilting frame which either lay on blocks or could be let down on ropes from the ceiling of a room. The latter was naturally more practical when one person or only a few people sat and worked. The quilting could be interrupted at any time without having to take the quilt off the frame, for when it was pulled up to the ceiling, the room could again be used without limitations. Round quilting frames, very much bigger and wider than embroidery hoops and yet functioning on the same principle of two circular forms one inside the other, came only much later.

Fabrics, Colors and Patterns: Early 19th Century

Very few of the quilts surviving today were signed or even dated. But if they do bear a signature in permanent ink, they must have been made since 1830.[117] The colorfast inks used earlier, which had to be stirred, destroyed the material and are scarcely legible today. Signing was also done in cross-stitching, naturally, but one must generally assume that very many signatures and dates were applied only later and therefore are only conditionally reliable.

It is impossible to date a quilt to a precise year of origin if it neither bears a reliable signature nor is handed down with some sort of documentation that can give evidence about its origin. Style, technique of working, fabrics and interlining allow dating reliable only to a quarter century at best. Fabrics and the styles that went with them are relatively reliable indications, even though one can never know how long the individual pieces of cloth may have lain in the sewing basket waiting to be used. For this reason, the newest cloth sewn into a patchwork gives the most truthful indication of the quilt's age. There are many very informative publications that explain the American textile industry and thus are a great help.[118] A characterization of what is notable about the materials of patchwork and applique quilts in America during the first half of the Nineteenth Century shall be attempted here.

The middle of the century forms a gap, then because before 1856 only natural colors were used to dye and print textiles, so forming their appearences.

Turkish red, a colorant developed in the Orient, is attained in a process of thirteen to twenty steps, and could be produced only after 1780 in England and 1829 in America. Despite this, Turkish red was extremely popular as a solid color for cotton textiles and as the background for flowered calicos, first as imported goods, and later in domestic production. All shades from a powerful bluish red to pink were possible, especially colorfast and very common in quilts before the Civil War. It is very hard to differentiate from the later red dyes.

An equally common dye, and one that was available for use, was indigo blue with its various light and dark shades. Like Turkish red, it is often found in Nineteenth-Century American quilts, and was used unchanged over long periods of time. But as identifying marks for dating, solid colors are not very useful, for their colors have changed only very little in the course of time, and they were not influenced by the dictates of fashion, as were the printed fabrics.

Only the green tones can give vague dating hints, since before the middle of the century there were only very mediocre dyes that soon faded from washing and light exposure. They remain today only as faded shadowings of brownish-gray, even though they were bright and clear when they were new. A strong yellow-green has been especially popular since about 1830, and often was seen in quilt styles. But in the end, cotton prints, calicos and chintzes that were preferred for use in the sewing of patchwork and appliques are much more informative than solid colors in helping to date quilts.

This can be illustrated very clearly using green as an example. Although it is the most commonly seen color in nature, it was not possible before 1815 to print it on fabrics in colorfast form. Blue and yellow had to be combined in two work processes. When the printing was off center, thin blue and yellow edges were singled at the left and right edge of the pattern. Even after 1815, when it was possible to print a colorfast green, one still finds fabrics with overprinted green in quilts made as late as the Forties. From 1830 to 1860 green appeared, particularly as a background for black or blue flower prints in combination with red, pink and yellow, in the very popular applique quilts with white backgrounds.

After 1815 the technique of drum printing spread in America, though only solid-color printing could be done with it before 1835. The colored motif was completed by hand with plate and block printing.

In the second quarter of the century, so-called rainbow or shadowed prints, with backgrounds varying from light to dark or from one color to another, became popular. A very special, vivid blue was especially common for this type of cloth. Flowers, birds, flourishes and architectural elements were popular motifs of the time. With the technical capability to print in several colors, designs developed with a richness of naturalistic details. Designs of dots, lines and small geometric patterns became just as popular as backgrounds for multicolored prints of small flowers as were bright reds and greens.

The variety of printed fabrics was inspired by the possibilities created through technical progress in the textile industry. At the beginning of the century, the patterns of block or plate printing were still imitated, monochrome red or blue patterns on white backgrounds, or black or white-outlined motifs on colored backgrounds. The drum printing process allowed much freedom from the previous technically limited designs, and around the middle of the century it

116

offered much opportunity to produce lively details and imaginative patterns in cotton prints. The American textile industry very soon was able to catch up and equal the progress of the European manufacturers, especially the English and French.

The tendency to use many shades of brown, especially in very old quilts, usually has relatively little to do with the fashions of the times. Colorfast dyeing and printing in all imaginable shades of brown could naturally be done at or even before the beginning of the century. Such fabrics were frequently used in quilts, but what looks pale brown, almost like a solid color to us today was often originally a bright color like purple, grass green or blue. Early shades of brown or black, on the other hand, often had a tendency to decay. This was due mainly to the chemical stains that were used for dyeing. In old calico quilts one often finds regularly spaced holes with the interlining showing through. These holes were once black or brown flowers or dots which have disintegrated completely.

The time of production of certain dyes, the popularity of certain colors and prints, as well as the dates of introducing special printing techniques all offer important information which can lead to placing a quilt realistically in terms of time and region. But since these factors are quite variable, even within one region, they must be examined anew for every quilt. The limiting of possibilities by the technical limitations of the first half of the Nineteenth Century turns in the second half to a variety that is almost impossible to deal with, as many new and different technical achievements were put into practice.

Fabrics, Colors and Patterns: Late 19th Century

More machines were available for the production of printed textiles after 1840. Equipped with several cylinders, they could print in more than one color. The invention of aniline colors by Perkin in 1856 completed the possibilities by providing an extensive palette of colorfast dyestuffs for textile printing. Thus the production of a great assortment of reasonably priced calicos became possible. They were patterned in considerable detail, with very fine shadowings and structurings of dots, lines and intricate little geometrical figures. Patterns were no longer limited to flowers and buds, leaves and birds. Sporting accessories such as whips, horseshoes, tennis rackets, bows and arrows, or sewing implements such as thimbles, needles and thread were used in textile patterns, along with other figures with a wide variety of subjects. So-called "eccentric fabrics" with strange geometric designs, crooked lines, zigzag or net patterns were especially popular. Portrayals of children were also printed in the style of Kate Greenaway illustrations,[119], as were strikingly natural-looking flies and other insects. Jubilee designs with small stars, stripes, Liberty Bells and the dates 1776-1876 took up themes of the time. Paisley in large and small scale, copper-red, brown and orange flowers and fruits, such as we associate with Provence prints today, set the style in the Seventies and Eighties.[120] Even patchwork was imitated in textile printing about 1850.

The wide variety of textile types and styles is so vast that one can scarcely survey them all. Typical of the second half of the Nineteenth Century are, above all, precision and realistic portrayal of motifs as well as abstract geometric patterns.

The pleasure found in the almost unlimited possibilities also found expression in the colorful nature of the fabrics. Above all, one sees very strong and true colors, subdued at most by a more or less thickly applied pattern.

Around the turn of the century a limitation of the colors to darker tones—dark red, navy blue, gray-blue, black, combined with gray, white and pink—can be seen. Patterns were limited to monochrome prints, either a print in solid color on a white background or white markings on a colored background. Though the patterns remained much the same, they were less detailed, less finely drawn. The variation consisted of their being set far apart, or thickly in stripes or serpentine lines. Black and white prints were the culmination of this sad and dreary choice of textiles. This development was brought on mainly by industry's efforts to produce more cloth more cheaply in a shorter time, which necessarily led to a loss of quality. And even the styles of the times were equally colorless in appearance. This tendency is reflected in turn-of-the-century quilts as well, though some quilters knew how to combine the dark shades with glowing colors such as hot pink or bright yellow, achieving splendid effects thereby.

At the same time, large-patterned chintzes were produced for interior decorating as well as fabrics for clothing in a wide variety of colors, details and patterns. The small-print calicos were intended for everyday clothing and dominated the appearance of patchwork quilts into the 1920»s. In addition, silk and velvet were also used in patchwork. They mark an individual patchwork style that expressed a growing prosperity.

Along with the many types of textiles came a variety of patchwork and applique styles that developed during the last half of the Nineteenth Century. Appliques on white backgrounds, with preferred combinations of red, green and yellow or orange, were very much in style into the Sixties. So-called "scrap quilts" became popular around 1870-1880. The material for these quilts was bought, swapped and collected with an eye to not having to use, if possible, two identical pieces in a patchwork—a bizarre way to increase the variety of the materials.

Along with pure calico quilts, silk mosaic patchworks and later crazy-quilts won the hearts of the patchwork makers.[121]

It is no longer possible to regard only a few basic quilt genres as typical of the second half of the Nineteenth Century, as it was in the first half with the "broderie perse quilts", applique quilts in medallion or block style and finally block-style patchwork quilts. The exchange of patchwork and applique patterns was no longer limited to small areas. Fashion magazines such as "Godey's Lady's Book",[122] "Peterson's" and others distributed them regardless of their origin, usually without even naming them.[123] These publications were directed mainly at women living in cities and had little to do with the needs of pioneer women in the country. Until 1850 it was mostly embroidery patterns that were printed; only in the latter half of the century were decorative patchwork patterns published. They were intended especially for silk patchwork, which was sewn in the English style, with "all-over" designs over paper patterns. These silk patchwork quilts and later crazy-quilts replaced the cotton applique quilts as elegant, decorative showpieces. With them, patchwork became a fashionable pastime of well-to-do ladies.

Only in the rural areas and in the West of the United States did the patchwork quilt continue without interruption to fulfill its popular function as a practical and beautiful object, and as such it was still made. The observation seems curious that during the Revolutionary War a high degree of independence was striven for even in the design of patchwork quilts, but after achieving these patriotic goals, this led back, at least in higher-class circles, led back to the decorative influence of the mother country. This phenomenon can probably be explained only in that styles were still dictated by Paris and London, and one had to follow them if one did not want to appear old-fashioned. This trend was also reinforced by magazines, and in the end it reached only those who were not greatly involved in keeping up with pioneering such as the women who had moved west with their men to start a new life. Just as the picture of Nineteenth-Century life in America must be drawn to include a lot of variety, so must that of its quilts.

Patchwork Patterns

Log Cabin

The technique of sewing patchwork implied by the use of geometric forms as patterns. The starting point was the bed, whose rectangular form set the basic pattern for the bedcover. Playing with colors and shapes finally produced the effect of a surface pattern and had much influence on the endless variations of simple to complicated compositions. Swallowed up by an "all-over" pattern, arranged in rows, in a checkerboard, in stripes or diagonals, the geometric elements were usually organized into a block pattern. In this way a maximum of practical use and decorative effect could be attained with a minimum of effort.[124]

The Log Cabin pattern is especially variable and has been very popular since the middle of the century. Its popularity does not depend on only practical and esthetic qualities. As a textile interpretation of the log cabin structure, which was so important to the pioneers in the West, this pattern of stripes translated the principles of log cabin building into cloth. These principles had been brought to the New World by Swedish immigrants as early as 1638. Like all other European concepts, whether functional or emotional, this Swedish technique was made to fit the new conditions, so that in the end a simple, clearly defined method of construction was developed for cabin builders and quilt makers alike. On their travels westward, the pioneers built log cabins chiefly as homes for their families and protection from the wilderness. Thus this cabin and the corresponding patchwork pattern became symbols of patriotic involvement, even when the women who sewed a log cabin quilt no longer had the firsthand experience of living on the edge of civilization. It amounted to an expression of solidarity with the people who had gone out to conquer the West and represented patriotic involvement.[125]

Traditional Log Cabin blocks, in contrast to earlier patchwork patterns, were usually sewn to a square piece of background cloth. A small square formed the center; its color, usually red, remained the same over the entire quilt, and symbolized the fireplace of the house, the hearth or stove. Around this square, the central source of light

75 Log Cabin "Barn Raising" Amish Plain City, Ohio, circa 1915, 191 x 186.
Verena Klüser Quilt Gallery, Munich, West Germany.

and warmth, the strips of cloth were sewn so that they projected into
each other. The block could be made, for example, as a square
diagonally divided into a light and a dark side. The combination of
the blocks allows a wide variety of strictly geometric and very
dynamic patterns. Along with the arrangement of the blocks, the
width of the stripes and the choice of fabrics form the individual
appearance of every Log Cabin quilt. At first home-woven and home-
dyed wool and linen cloth was used, later cotton prints, and finally
silk and velvet. The practical advantage of Log Cabin patchwork was
certainly not just that one could use up scraps of cloth, but also the
opportuniy to use them unquilted and unstuffed.

To name the patterns, the women often drew on important
elements of life in the wilderness, and these names remained with the
Log Cabin quilts that were made in cities and on the East Coast. A
diamond shape spreading over the entire quilt in light-dark contrasts
bears the name "Barn Raising" (#75). It refers to the gatherings of the

76 Log Cabin "Pineapple" Mennonite, Pennsylvania, circa 1870, 212 x 185. Verena Klüser Quilt Gallery, Munich, West Germany.

settlers, so important in their social interaction, in which they gave each other emotional support as well as practical help, in order to be able to overcome the difficulties inherent in settling the western territories.

Diagonals in light and dark shades, running across the whole surface of the quilt, were called "Straight Furrow" and symbolized a farmer's plowed fields and rows of crops, as well as the hard work of the pioneers in producing fruit from the soil they had first made arable.

"Zig Zag", "Streak of Lightning" or "Running Fence" are the possible names of a striking zigzag pattern. These names also refer to everyday phenomena of the settlers' lives, whether the thunder and lightning of a storm or the bordering and securing of one's own property. Both were important enough to inspire a name. The same is true of the many windmills so often stylized in patchwork patterns, particularly of the Log Cabin type (#78).

77 Log Cabin of English clothing fabrics, circa 1860, 203 x 203. American Museum in Britain, Claverton Manor, Bath, UK.

There were many chances to relate the emerging patterns to everyday life—even if they didn't absolutely need to be related. "Courthouse Steps" or "Pineapple" (#76) are good examples of this. Their background square shows a different arrangement of colors from the variations we have already mentioned. The stripes that taper in to the center from four or eight directions intersect to form flights of stairs. "Pineapple" was always a symbol of hospitality, and was very popular for that reason.[125]

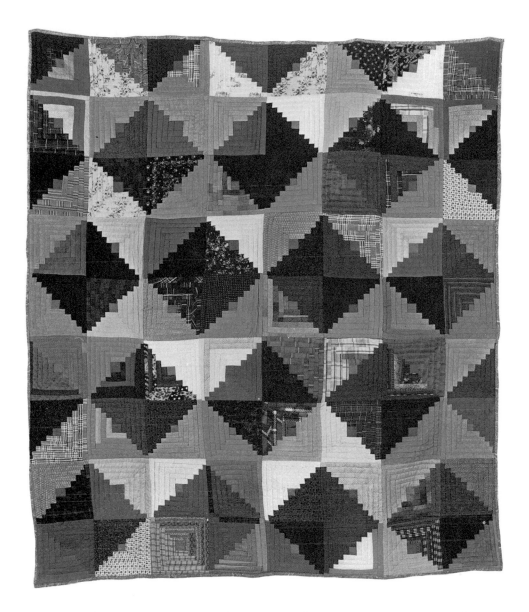

78 Log Cabin of woolen fabrics, from the Washington area, circa 1880, 197 x 180.
Atef-Schreiterer Collection, Berlin, West Germany.

Log Cabin must be regarded as one of the best-loved patchwork patterns of the latter half of the Nineteenth Century, which makes it difficult to associate with the patriotic ideals of the time. One need only think of decorative Log Cabin bedcovers in the houses of well-off bourgeois city dwellers. There bright rows and bands of taffeta were used along with velvet, silk and brocade, often in contrast to black satin. But even these splendid variations look especially well in the Log Cabin pattern (#77).

79 Sunburst quilt by Rebecca Scattergood Savery, Pennsylvania, 1835-1840, 317 x 301. Museum of American Folk Art, New York, USA.

Stars as Patchwork Patterns

Since the end of the Eighteenth Century, the star motif has been the undoubted favorite among patchwork patterns. It can be found in over a hundred different variations of form and contrasting effects. In the book, "Romance of the Patchwork Quilt in America", by Carrie Hall and Rose Kretsinger, ninety different star patterns are illustrated.

The star, as symbol and source of light, has always stimulated man's imagination. As a Christian symbol of hope and promise, it has stood more or less for harmony and expressed in one way or

80 Star of Bethlehem, Quilt. Museum of the City of Alzey, West Germany.

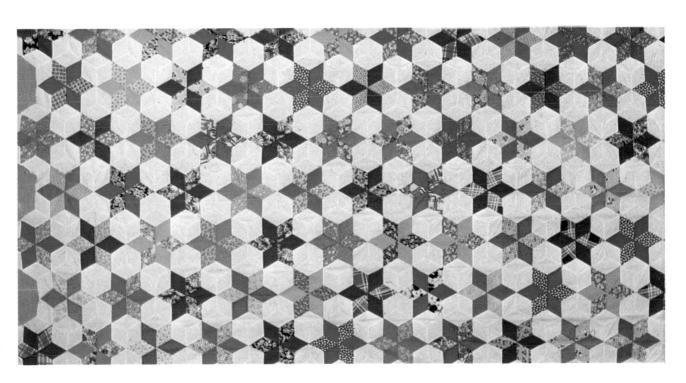

81 Patchwork top, "Le Moyne Star", circa 1930, 250 x 202. Privately owned by Rosa Dames, Berlin, West Germany.

another, especially emphatically, the aspirations of the pioneers in the New World. Along with the primary positive symbolism of the star or pattern of stars, there almost seems to be a secondary significance as well, whether the name was taken from nature, religion or politics. The different names of the same stars, or the same name given to different stars, were usually significant in regional terms, and in the rarest of cases can it be called on today. Only the thoroughly optimistic content has remained unchanged and effectively relevant over the generations. As an example of the Americans' preference for the star symbol in exposed places stands the national flag of the United States, where a star represents every state of the union.

The star offered its shape for use in patchwork quilts in an endless variety of possible patterns. From a single central motif that dominates the whole exposed side of the quilt (Star of Bethlehem, #80, Blazing Star, Broken Star) to a row of more intricate, small patterns (Variable Star), from the combination of large and small stars (Star of Bethlehem with Le Moyne Star) to patterns of groups of stars (The Seven Stars of the Pleiades)[126] or as four or six large individual stars (Touching Stars), all variations were popular. Every star patchwork pattern, aside from its decorative qualities, was made as an expression of the women's special hopes and good wishes.

The basic forms of all patchwork stars are diamonds and squares in various arrangements and in combination with triangles of all kinds. Their variety is increased by the endless possibilities of combining contrasting colors. The favorite star pattern that challenged a seamstress' skill the most was the eight-pointed "Le Moyne Star" (#81) made of triangles. It was named after the Le Moyne brothers, who founded the city of New Orleans in 1718, and in New England it was also called the "Star of Le Moyne" or the "Lemon Star". Since 1793 it has been accepted as a definite patchwork pattern, from which many lovely star variations have developed over the years.[127] Its six-pointed relative, also formed of diamonds, is the "Morning Star".[128] In the pattern known as the "Star of Bethlehem", "Blazing Star", "Star of the East" or "Broken Star", the central eight-pointed star was developed into large stars extending over the whole quilt. They stand out from light or dark backgrounds in particularly bright and vivid color combinations. Smaller patchwork stars, appliqued motifs of flora and fauna, and particularly finely sewn quilting patterns usually accompany these splendid stars in the open fields around them and on the strips of edging. That particularly popular "explosion of color" in which hundreds of diamond-shaped patches radiate from the eight-pointed central star to the borders in a gigantic wheel is called a "Sunburst" (#79). The greatest precision was required to make stars of diamonds, for any imprecision that crept in

82 Patchwork quilt with the "Feathered Star" pattern developed into the "Variable Star", late Nineteenth Century, 259 x 208. American Museum in Britain, Claverton Manor, Bath, UK.

while cutting or sewing the pieces multiplied in its extent as the star grew. If the angles and edges did not match exactly, then a bulge developed in the middle and the edge developed folds, so that the whole quilt could not be spread out flat. One tried to avoid these difficulties by sewing the pieces very precisely over paper patterns. But to this day countless patchwork fragments of the "Star of Bethlehem" have survived, unfinished because of a tiny error.[129]

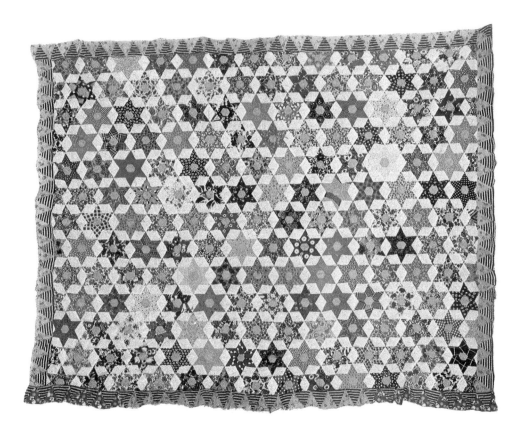

83 Patchwork top, "Texas Star", and a detail of the pattern, circa 1930, 235 x 180. Privately owned by Rosa Dames, Berlin, West Germany.

Detail of #83.

84 Mariner's Compass quilt, Pennsylvania, circa 1850, 264 x 264. American Museum in Britain, Claverton Manor, Bath, UK.

Since 1775 the "Variable Star" has been known as a patchwork pattern.[130] Set into a square block, this eight-pointed star is formed of a central square and eight triangles. It is much easier to sew than the "Star of Le Moyne" and almost as popular. Though it is used now and then to dominate a patchwork quilt as a large single motif, it is used much more frequently as a block, alternating with solid-color blocks, in edges or corners. Surrounded by a stripe made of small triangles in a contrasting color, it becomes the "Feathered Star" (#82). Most star variations are developed from the constructive principle of the "Variable Star" by changing the proportions of the individual elements to each other or by enclosing the central star with additional zigzag edges. Pentagons and hexagons form the origin for five- and six-pointed stars.[131] The variety of these stars cannot be illustrated adequately but is reflected in a vast array of star quilts that have survived in great numbers since the middle of the Nineteenth Century (#83).

The "Mariner's Compass", also known as the "Sunburst", "Sunrising" or "Sunflower", belongs in this company as a special form of the star motif.[132] The original inspiration for this pattern may well have been the compass roses on old sea charts, that were developed into patchwork or applique patterns particularly by women in coastal areas. Consisting of no fewer than four and no more than thirty-two very slim, pointed rays running together, usually around a circle or a hexagon, this pattern demanded outstandingly skilled handiwork in design and sewing. Here too the paper inlay was a useful aid in sewing patchwork or applique. The difference in name between "Mariner's Compass", which regardless of its number of rays always has four main rays perpendicular to each other, or a star or sun name, was left in the end to the subjective evaluation of the quiltmaker or observer (#84).

Still in all, the suggestion was made that the difference be systematized in terms of technique, in that the sewn-together motif be called "Mariner's Compass" and the appliqued pattern be called a star or sun.[133] This example shows clearly how difficult it is to categorize the various star motifs definitively. The question arises of whether there is any sense to such efforts. It is probably quite meaningless to the makers of patchwork. Popular patterns have definite names thanks to their widespread and frequent use known to everyone, such as "Star of Bethlehem". Other stars bore names that were obvious when one looked at them, such as "Feathered Star", "Broken Star" or "Touching Stars". But most names are based on fanciful associations, and perhaps the description of the star pattern types above will suffice to help one find one's way among the many forms in which patchwork stars appear.

Friendship and Album Quilts

Since 1830 the move into the West of North America increased under the pressure of the waves of immigrants from Europe. The pioneer women who moved westward with their men over the Appalachians and Alleghenies in search of a new basis of existence were helped by the growing numbers of so-called women's magazines published since the early 1830»s. These often served for long periods of time as their only links to the civilization they had left. "Godey's Lady's Book Magazine" was probably the most popular magazine of this kind, which published not only fashion news, embroidery patterns and other information on handicrafts, cooking recipes and household hints, but also stories, poems and songs. The individual issues were read over and over, collected and handed on.

A part of the pioneering spirit which in almost all families meant parting from close relatives and friends, was a spirit of friendship that found romanticized expression above all in the women's magazines. This spirit was also expressed in the widespread keeping of poetry albums, in which true friendship was expressed by poetic entries, which could be formulated appropriately under the influence of the verses and rhymes from "Godey's Lady's Book Magazine". Following this style, American women sewed friendship quilts, which were particularly popular between 1840 and 1875.[134] They were similar in appearance to the ordinary everyday quilts whose patchwork blocks were made of colorful cotton cloth, scraps from clothing and the like (#86). But in the blocks of friendship quilts there was always a white field reserved for inscriptions. At the of their popularity, in the Forties and Fifties, these friendly dedications consisted not just of name, place and date, but also of verses, expressions of love and good wishes, which were inspired in form quite obviously by magazines and poetry albums. Even notations of age, or of the birth or death of a child, were made. With fountain pen or quill and indelible ink, in script or printing, the words were written on the cloth. In areas of Maryland, Pennsylvania and New Jersey it was also very popular to hide the name amid fine, detailed drawings of leaves, vases, flowers, birds and fountains. In the Sixties and Seventies the dedications were finally reduced to the names, often only the initials, to which were

85 Baltimore Bridal Quilt by Alice A. Ryder, 1847, 314 x 314. American Museum in Britain, Claverton Manor, Bath, UK.

added at most the place and date. The signature was usually embroidered, and made much larger and more noticeable than before. Entries made with a hand-stamp were also common.

The feeling of friendship which one expressed in an entry on a friendship quilt certainly did not decrease in the course of time. But the changes that occurred in patchwork quilting as a whole during the second half of the Nineteenth Century are seen particularly clearly in friendship quilts. The effects of the Civil War brought a mood of sorrow, and when the war was over, the popularity of the friendship quilt declined in favor of other patchwork styles, such as the crazy-quilt.

There were many ways to make a friendship quilt, and the maker could choose her own rules. She could sew the blocks herself, enter the names on them and sew them together, and have family or friends

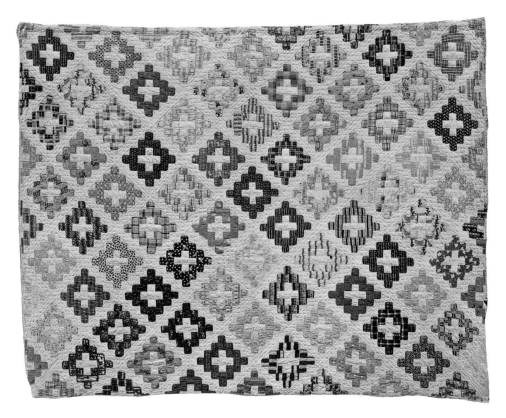

86 *Friendship quilt, "Chimney Sweep", with detail, Connecticut, circa 1840. Privately owned by Dorle Stern Straeter, Munich.*

Detail of #86.

help with the quilting. This method was especially appropriate when a woman made a patchwork out of a dead person's clothing as a memorial. It was also possible to distribute the white pieces to friends and relatives and ask them to sign them. Naturally this was done with exact instructions as to the form in which it had to be done to create a uniform pattern. It was also her job to sew and assemble the blocks. Ultimately the situation could progress to the point where only the chosen patchwork pattern was announced, whereupon everyone who wanted to be immortalized in the quilt sewed the block in her own fabrics. Despite the multitude of possibilities, it is noticeable that the results are very similar regardless of time and place. Particularly suitable standard patterns for friendship quilts developed over the years, such as "The Chimney Sweep" or "Album Patch". But any other popular patchwork pattern, such as Log Cabin, Nine-Patch variations or stars, would have done just as well, and yet they were chosen much more rarely.

The meaning and value of a friendship quilt normally equalled the sentimental appeal of a poetry album. If the remains of an article of the beloved person's clothing were worked into the quilt, that naturally increased the value even more. Women sewed friendship quilts for themselves, and it could take years before the many collected dedications or blocks were assembled; or they made them as parting gifts or mementos for dear relatives and friends. Though very much like everyday quilts in appearance and construction, they were very much more sparely quilted as they were not used. Being decorative mementos, they usually lay in a hope chest, or on a bed as a decorative cover. Very seldom does one find examples that were decorated nearly as thoroughly with quilting patterns as their "rich relations", the album quilts.

The elegant album quilts,[135] that reached the height of their popularity at the same time as the friendship quilts, were made for the same reasons (#87). They may have been more closely linked with specific events: wedding gifts to the bride from her friends, freedom quilts for a young man's twenty-first birthday, gifts to express thanks to the community's pastor, mementos for a parting friend, souvenirs of certain regional historical events, and so on. There were plenty of themes and symbols to be portrayed in applique or patchwork technique, using colorful cotton cloth on white squares. These signed blocks, usually made and signed by various women, were arranged in a grid of horizontal and vertical rows. In communal work the assembled cover was quilted with geometric or other patterns to complete the appliqued motifs.

The appliques, and more rarely patchwork, were made of solid-color and patterned cottons, calicos and decorative chintzes. Either entire printed patterns were used, such as flowers or birds in

87 Album quilt from Vermont, with detail, 1870, 220x220. Badisches Landes Museum, Karlsruhe, West Germany

Detail of #87.

"broderie perse" style, or the motifs were cut out and applied through careful use of the cloth patterns and structures. So-called rainbow patterns or small scattered patterns on a dominating colored background did much to bring the pictures to life. The comparison with appliques which were sewn out of solid-colored fabrics and had a more subdued effect makes the difference clear. The degree of realistic portrayal depended on the individual seamstress's talent and experience in working with cloth. For example Mary Evans Ford or Achsa Godwin Wilkins of Baltimore were so talented and famous that they sewed whole album quilts and also individual blocks for others commercially. The "Pennsylvania Dutch" women, on the other hand, very deliberately preferred a stylized form of expression that was more related to the traditions of German folk art, but not necessarily less decorative.[136] Many of their flower and leaf motifs, as well as human and animal figures, are reminiscent of the picturesque scenes on Bohemian patchwork coverlets of the Eighteenth Century. Motifs may also have had their sources in old paper-cutting patterns. Within these extremes there developed the greatest variety of styles, which were characterized by the individual's talent for handiwork. In the end, all album quilts, whether they were made in Maryland or Ohio, looked similar at first glance in terms of construction and use of color. Such deviations from the basic system as the formation of a diagonally arranged grid or the layout of a central motif seem to be individual decisions rather than generally accepted goals.[137]

Naturally, flowers are the main motif of album quilts—in vases, baskets, horns of plenty, in bouquets, wreaths and hearts. Many kinds of leaf motifs, branches and vines, as well as birds and butterflies were added as decorative elements. The same floral motifs are found on applique quilts during the latter half of the century. These quilts, in the clearly dominating colors of red and green on white backgrounds, had come into fashion as showpieces around 1850. Most of them display rows of identical flower or vine patterns, and generally they are quilted very finely. This type of quilt was also made in patchwork, in such patterns as the "Carolina Lily". Though in these quilts it was repetition that created the appealing form, variety did the job in album quilts, where normally no block was duplicated. Correspondingly, the tradition of picturesque scenes, which often enough gave the impetus to make the quilt, was repeated in album quilts. Emblems in the most unusual combinations, architecture and historical monuments, means of transportation such as trains and ships, and even books such as the bible or a poetry album found their place in these colorful quilts.

The center that produced the album quilts recognized as the most beautiful in the 1840's and 1850's was the city of Baltimore, Maryland. Here it was mainly Methodist women who specialized in making them (#85). Since many have survived and are of unique quality, their complex social-historical background has been studied in depth. Thanks to their signatures, as compared with other documents, the lives of the women who made them have become better known, at least in part. The themes portrayed on many blocks have had very clear connections to noteworthy events in the city's history. All this gives the quilts an immeasurable documentary value. The city of Baltimore recognized this fact in 1982 with a display of twenty-four Baltimore album quilts—a richness of quilts in the same style that could scarcely be equalled to this extent in any one region for any other genre of quilts of equally outstanding quality.

Crazy Quilts

In the days when it was popular, crazy patchwork was also known as puzzle patchwork or Japanese patchwork.[138] But it was best known as crazy, either in the sense of 'insane' or that of 'smashed up' like the irregular shards of a broken piece of ceramic.

Crazy quilts were made out of irregular pieces, usually of very costly fabrics, and decorated with ornamental stitching and motifs. Despite their name, the layers of crazy quilts were not quilted, but only tacked or tied, for the fabrics used were usually too thick to sew through in the way required for a quilting pattern.

For a long time it was claimed that sewing pieces of cloth together without choosing their shapes was the original patchwork technique, and that the first North American settlers had made such quilts. This thesis was probably advanced by Ruth Finley.[139] She believed that this technique must have been very widespread at a time when every bit of cloth had to be imported from Europe and every scrap of it was too valuable to be wasted. Many authors have accepted this theory, but it has proved to be untenable. There is no surviving example of a crazy quilt or other definite evidence from the early colonial era. Crazy patchwork surely must be regarded as an American invention in the Victorian Age.

In the latter half of the Nineteenth Century, wool and cotton quilts were regarded as old-fashioned. Since the manufacture of silk was expanding in North America at this time, and the costly material was becoming more affordable, it was considered chic to sew silk patchwork.[140] Women's magazines and instruction books supported this trend, partiaularly promoting the English pattern technique for silk patchwork (#89).[141] But the Log Cabin pattern also attained new honors in silk, for working with the contrasts of dark and glowing colors was much loved. But in the Seventies these elegant covers were pushed out of the picture by crazy quilts, just as the ordinary cotton quilts had been previously—both were regarded in America as not artistic enough.

Japanese art and culture were displayed to a hitherto unknown extent at the expositions of 1862 in London and 1876 in Philadelphia. The Japanese Pavilion in Philadelphia drew 9.5 million visitors and was the most successful stand in the fair. Japanese styles immediately became the latest fashionable and influenced wallpaper, textiles, interior decoration, accessories and literature.[142] Women showed their eagerness to experiment with the new styles and inspirations in crazy patchwork, in both quilts and useful items from slippers to pillows (#88). These things fit perfectly into the interior decor of the time, with its heavy fabrics and dark wood, upholstered furniture and endless knick-knacks. The interest in making one's home look artistic was part of an esthetic movement that came from England in

88 House slippers with "fancy work", England, end of the 19th Century. Museum of Costumes and Textiles, Nottingham, UK.

89 Tumbling Cubes coverlet, England, 1910-1930, 150 x 100. Privately owned by Barbara and Paul Clemens, Cologne, West Germany.

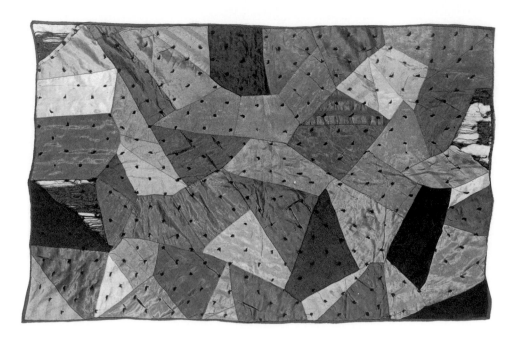

90 Crazy quilt, Maryland, circa 1910, 160 x 160. Atef-Schreiterer Collection, Berlin, West Germany.

the Sixties under the leadership of such artists as John Ruskin and William Morris. It was believed that a beautiful home had a good effect on the morality and productivity of its inhabitants. In addition, the ideal prevailed of making something beautiful out of 'nothing', and every woman who cared about herself and her good reputation busied herself in making artistically valuable useful things out of all imaginable materials.[143]

This striving seems to have been just as widespread in the country as in the large cities, even though the available materials looked a bit different. It goes almost without saying that this whole movement was supported by women's magazines and the new publications on art and decoration[144] in great detail, with suggestions, instructions, stories, poems, hints for having crazy tea parties and laying out flowerbeds in crazy style.

The formative principle of crazy patchwork had the goal of creating the most colorful, varied and lavish effect possible (#90, 92). The forming of straight lines and neat angles was to be avoided whenever possible. The patches were sewn onto a background, beginning with a first piece around which all the others were placed, in what resembled the Log Cabin style. The background either had its final size or was cut as a block or stripe. Planning a crazy quilt for decorative effect in the style of a medallion quilt, with an emphasized central motif, as with Log Cabin or album quilts, was about as common as arranging the pieces in a regular grid of diamonds, hexagons or other geometric forms.

One generally made a crazy quilt for oneself or for sale. But they could be inspired by the same impulses that led to the making of a cotton quilt: baptism, marriage, parting and thanks, remembrance of beloved people or events. Crazy quilts were usually much smaller than other quilts and were regarded purely as decoration, without any practical value. Then too, the mixture of different materials did not allow them to be washed.

91 Fan quilt of woolen cloth, circa 1930. Atef-Schreiterer Collection, Berlin, West Germany.

92 Patriotic crazy quilt from Pennsylvania, circa 1889, 193 x 147. H. M. Klinger House of Art, Nuremberg, West Germany.

Along with the scraps that remained when new clothes were made, cloth was also exchanged among friends and relatives to attain as colorful a palette of different cloth qualities and colors as possible. Bundles of silk scraps could be ordered by mail from textile factories, and the pattern books of textile dealers were much in demand. It was

93 Hardmann medallion quilt, New York City, end of the 19th Century. The Haggin Museum, Stockton, California, USA.

regarded as especially original to work into one's quilts such things as cigarette or cigar wrappings, taffeta ribbons, pennants and small flags, leftover bits of lace, and much more, with the most varying patterns or even printed lettering. Around 1884, at the height of the crazy style, there were even regular kits on the market, offering pieces already cut for specific crazy-quilt patterns.

Along with the wide variety of form, color and material in individual pieces, embroidery emerged as the dominant decorative element of crazy quilts. Solid-colored fields or embroidered, appliqued or painted motifs were surrounded by decorative stitching in contrasting colors. In addition, borders, piping and pearls were worked into English crazy quilts (#93).

The motifs were generally made according to patterns in magazines and books; only very seldom were they designed by the women themselves. For this reason, the same motifs are found again and again in quilts from widely separated regions. Most popular were portrayals of Japanese flowers, animals and objects: iris, cherry blossoms and chrysanthemums, cranes amid reeds, owls and peacocks, flying swallows, spiders in webs, insects and beautiful butterflies, fans, vases and paper lanterns. Along with fashionable details one sees Kate Greenaway figures and domestic animals and plants. The flower motifs were to a certain degree like those of the applique patterns of traditional quilts, with the difference that they could be made much more realistic by embroidery. A "language of flowers" was very widespread, by which hidden messages could be expressed in the arrangement of specific flowers.[145]

At the end of the Nineteenth Century, the strong wave of crazy-quilt style ebbed almost as spontaneously as it had risen. People looked again to the good qualities of traditional cotton quilts, which were made in the Seventies and Eighties almost exclusively in rural areas. By 1910 the interest in crazy quilts had almost died. Where they were still made, these corvers that once looked so splendid and extravagant developed more and more into practical quilts of wool or cotton. The embroidery vanished too, for the sake of making them more useful (#91).

In the end, the crazy quilt was left with nothing but its significance in cultural history as a fashionable fad of the ending Nineteenth Century, vividly illustrating the spirit of the times in a clearly defined epoch.[146]

Amish Quilts

Among all the patchwork made by American settler women in the Nineteenth Century, the quilts of the Amish sect take an outstanding position. Their appearance almost ideally represents, in form and color, the standards of modern conceptions of art, particularly those of the Pop Art and Minimal Art movements of the 1960»s. For that very reason, the Amish quilts enjoy a very great popularity among collectors today. Along with these parallels, which in the end amount to a chance closeness to present-day taste, the quality of handiwork in Amish quilts is just as remarkable as their simple and yet so dynamic formation out of reduced geometric forms and brilliant, extraordinary combinations of colors. The basic reason why Amish quilts strike the eye as different from all other American patchwork styles derives from the particular way of belief and life of the Amish sect.

The Amish have their roots in the religious community of the Mennonites. This group broke away from the Protestant Reformed Church during the Sixteenth Century under the leadership of Menno Simons, because their conceptions of their goals went beyond those of the church. The Mennonites, as did the Amish later, stood for the baptism of adults, the separation of church and state, and the rejection of military service, oaths and divorce. Following Christ in the sense of the Sermon on the Mount was to them an obligatory way of life, and therefore they were persecuted by both Catholic and Protestant rulers. During the Sixteenth Century, they found refuge in The Netherlands and West Prussia, and after the Thirty Years' War also in South Germany. Since 1683, emigration to America offered them a way out. The State of Pennsylvania, founded by the Quaker William Penn in 1682, granted all persecuted peoples the freedom of religion. And in Germany a group under the Mennonite preacher Jacob Amman broke off in 1693, believing that Mennonite life had not separated sufficiently from all worldly things. This group, known as Amish, differs from the Menonites to this day not so much in basic belief as in stricter life style and discipline.[147] The first Amish came to America around 1727; others followed during the Eighteenth Century and again between 1830 and 1850.[148]

94 Diamond in Square quilt, Amish, Lancaster County, circa 1890, 200 x 194. Verena Klüser Quilt Gallery, Munich, West Germany.

95 Bars Quilt, Amish, Lancaster County, circa 1880, 214 x 193. Verena Klüser Quilt Gallery, Munich, West Germany.

148

96 Carpenter's Square quilt, Mennonite, Lancaster County, 1929-30, 198 x 198. Verena Klüser Quilt Gallery, Munich, West Germany.

The center of their first settlements was Lancaster County, Pennsylvania. where the most conservative of these sects, the "Old Order Amish", live to this day. Later they moved westward to Mifflin County, Pennsylvania, and finally over the state line to the west, to Ohio, Indiana, Illinois, Missouri, Iowa and Canada. Community life in the newer settlements is never as strictly led as in Lancaster, and one can speculate as to whether the groups moved away to other regions because of disagreement.[149]

In their communal life as farmers and craftsmen in country settlements and villages, the Amish try to separate themselves geographically and culturally from their neighbors and thereby from the malicious temptations of the world.

Among their neighbors were Quakers and Mennonites, who are counted among the "plain Dutch". Those German immigrants who did not belong to any sect were called "gay Dutch".[150] These last accepted the spiritual and material joys of life and expressed them creatively in colorful applique quilts. Their typical motifs, such as stylized tulips or birds, are rich in memories of German folk art.[151]

Since the Amish always did business with the "English" in their areas, they naturally could not withdraw completely. But they preferred contact with the Quakers and Mennonites, who were closer to them in belief and outer appearance. Where many Amish settlements lay close together, as in Lancaster County, the outside influences were not as effective as in the communities farther west, who often settled far apart and needed to maintain more intensive contact with the "English". The idea of making patchwork quilts, though, was "of the world", belonging to the life style of the "English", and was taken up by Amish women around 1860 in their own style. The Amish quilts of the traditional type were made mainly between 1870 and 1935—they are often very hard to date because of the similarity of their patterns and exclusive use of unpatterned cloth. The solid-color fabrics used for their patchwork was dyed at home with plant colors during the Nineteenth Century and during World War I, or at times with commercial dyes. Since the end of the last century there have been stores that stocked textiles to meet the particular wishes of the Amish. The patchwork parts were usually sewn by machine from the very start, unless children or grandmothers could be trusted with this work. As interlining they used raw uncombed wool, and the backs could be of cotton cloth with small checkered or flowered patterns. In the Twenties and Thirties there were more and more backs were made of other fabrics such as flowered flannel, which were warmer and lighter.[152] Quilting was done by hand communally, and the finest, most beautiful examples come from the turn of the century, when cotton and wool were the preferred materials. Since the Forties the Amish have not avoided using rayon and dacron textiles as well as synthetic fleece, which has lowered the quality of their quilts.

It can be said in general that the intricacy and brightness of the Amish quilts increased in the course of time. In the most conservative and at the same time most prosperous Amish communities of Lancaster County the simplest quilts were made (#94). To make the traditional, very simplified central motifs such as "Center Square", "Diamond in Square" and "Bars", the women seem to have chosen textiles especially for quilt making, for the large pieces could scarcely have been scraps (#95). Despite this, they stuck to the colors that were accepted, for clothing as well. Children and young women wore bright blue, green, purple, pink and dark red, which were combined with the deep mixed colors and earth colors reserved exclusively for older people. The center was usually enclosed by several inner borders and corner squares in contrasting colors, the "cornerstone",[153] and an identical stripe of edging. This type of quilt had already appeared in the linsey-woolsey quilts of the late Eighteenth and early Nineteenth Centuries. They left a particular lot of space for varied quilt patterns, and the Amish preferred the different formations of radiant eight-pointed stars or the feather wreath as a central motif. Flowers and leaves surrounded it. Garlands of feathers, leaves and grapevines as well as entwined geometric motifs and diamond patterns cover the space that remains free and the strips of edging. Many quilt motifs are very similar to the applique patterns of the 'gay Dutch", though they are more restrained and do not break the spirit of "order".[154]

As the Amish see it, a quilt should be above all a useful object, for decorations and ornaments are a sign of excess, which they avoid. Their houses too are clean and cheerily colorful, but without any needless accessories. Here, as in their patchwork, they limit themselves to the necessities, which led to limitation to the point of abstraction in the designing of their quilts. Through unusual combinations of colors that are not so sensational in themselves, Amish quilts became that which many have tried to describe but one must see for oneself. In this respect one has spoken of the "vivid aggressiveness of colors that reflects the vividness of their faith."[155]

The "Sunshine and Shadow" pattern made of many small squares (and known in non-Amish circles as "Trip Around the World"), or the eight-pointed "Lone Star" (known elsewhere as "Star of Bethlehem"), as well as its "Broken Star" variation, along with the countless block patterns that the Amish adopted over the years, did not merely provide opportunities to use up scraps of cloth (#96). They offered a purpose-linked chance to play with colors that was accepted especially in the poorer Amish areas of the West. Inspired by their neighbors in their search for new forms to use, the Amish women of Ohio and Indiana made their quilts brighter and brighter. The use of black as a contrast to glowing colors is particularly typical of their work.[156] Concrete patchwork motifs like "Basket", "Schoolhouse" and many others were made, even though they would scarcely have fit into the old concept of "order" if this had not been somewhat liberalized. In the end, all kinds of quilt patterns found a home with the Amish, even crazy quilts being sewn in Lancaster and Mifflin Counties of Pennsylvania.[157]

With the increasing intricacy of patterns and the growing experience of the Amish women, the variety of colors grew and the strictness of form decreased. Finally the Amish even used patterned cloth in their patchwork quilts, which only the Mennonites had been allowed to do previously. Today they produce almost exclusively for sale to tourists, and their quilts do not always represent just what can be described as typically Amish.

Afro-American Quilts

Little attention has been given until now, particularly in the literature, to the patchwork quilts of black Americans. Those who know them consider it possible, though, that in the future they will win the rank of greatest popularity among collectors away from the Amish quilts.[158] The Afro-American quilts cannot, though, be described as a single phenomenon, as the Amish quilts can. On the basis of their varied historical origins and forms of appearance, it makes sense to divide them into four groups,[159] in order to describe their basic points.

First come those quilts that were made during the existence of slavery in the southern states by black slave women who served as seamstresses and nursemaids on the plantations. They made quilts in the traditional patterns that had been taught to them, and attained a high degree of perfection. These quilts were recognized as valuable by their owners and handed down within the family.[160] It even seems to have been customary to have the slaves do particularly complex and demanding work such as trapunto, so that even simple patchwork would be made more valuable thereby.[161] Such quilts were actually made to standards that made them indistinguishable from others in terms of style and technique. In addition, now and then they were signed falsely. In few cases is the work of slaves on them attested to in writing.

152

97 Log Cabin variations with applique, New Jersey, circa 1870, 193 x 157. American Antiques and Quilts, Thomas K. Woodward, New York, USA.

It is simpler to recognize the specific type of Afro-American quilt with ethnological roots that are obvious in its outward appearance. Although the blacks in America were systematically robbed of their culture over the centuries, remains of African culture show up clearly in them.

On the one hand, there are applique quilts whose motifs are not very realistic but full of symbolism. A beautiful and very well-known example is the quilt, "The Creation of the Animals", made by the former slave Harriet Powers of Athens, Georgia, which she displayed at a country fair in 1886 (#98). A white teacher named Jennie Smith bought it in 1890, after Harriet Powers had explained the meaning of the individual scenes to her. For example, "the day the stars fell", November 12, 1833, is portrayed. On that day a meteor shower lasted for eight hours, and many believed the Day of Judgment had come and this was the rain of fire that would destroy the world. The slaves regarded this day as a fixed date from which to reckon all important events such as births and deaths of close friends. The "Black Friday" of May 19, 1780, on which devastating forest fires broke out in New England, is also portrayed. At that time Harriet Powers had not yet been born, but she certainly must have heard about the frightening event.[162] The type of appliqued figures and animals is clearly reminiscent of appliqued textile motifs from Dahomey, West Africa. How direct a line may be drawn to the possible origins of such forms of expression has thus far remained unclear—even though they are obvious.

On the other hand, there are patchwork quilts that clearly reflect the constructive techniques of African textiles. They are called stripe or band quilts. Full of color, and often with asymmetrically arranged patterns, they particularly suggest a remote relationship with West African narrow-band weaves, especially in terms of how they are used.[163]

In this very special context, one must certainly consider the development of a patchwork technique by the Seminole Indians in Florida at the end of the Nineteenth Century. Out of very simple earlier applique forms the Seminole women developed a structural patchwork. Long strips were sewn together into many-colored bands which were cut into many pieces and then assembled according to preconceived plans into strips with geometric patterns. Combined with different patterns or strips of solid colors, this patchwork was made into clothing with horizontal rows. Slaves from the Southern states who escaped often found refuge with the Seminole Indians, who took them in and sometimes intermarried with them. The blacks were known for their own stripe quilts, and the African influence doubtless served to inspire the Indians.[164]

98 Applique quilt, "The Creation of the Animals', by Harriet Powers, made in Athens, Georgia, 1895-1898, 266 x 175. Museum of Fine Arts, Boston, USA.

Many of the Afro-American women made quilts with characteristic patterns that link them more with African textiles than with the traditional Euro-American quilts. Normally the pattern is of more importance than the handiwork. The effect from a distance was most important. In West Africa it was chiefly the kings and priests who dressed in textiles with vivid patterns that had symbolic meanings and took on the character of status symbols. Even at some distance their strong colors gave the correct signal to those who approached them. The patchwork quilts of the black Americans can also be interpreted in this sense of cultural continuity, even though the political and economic situation was completely different. The variety of patterns, though, still plays an important esthetic role. And even though the motifs have long come from the Euro-American tradition, the particular arrangement of colors and forms can give the viewer a hint that suggests an Afro-American patchworker (#97).[165] At the same time, there are many quilts that were sewn by black women but show no trace of ethnological difference. Here the seamstresses took over the Euro-American patchwork traditions unchanged without feeling creatively hemmed in.

Finally there remain those quilts that were made by white women using specifically black themes. The way whites regarded blacks was particularly subordinated to the spirit of the times, and is reflected correspondingly drastically in the quilts of the various eras. Before the Civil War the women had invented certain patchwork blocks that referred to slavery. "Slave Chain", "Underground Railroad" or "Radical Rose" are patterns marked with a deep involvement in the fate of the slaves. They take on an even more emphatic meaning when one considers that women of those times were damned to at least official neutrality. But even in quilts they found ways to express their political positions. It is striking that there are considerably fewer suggestions of approval of slavery in patchwork quilts.

With the growing industrialization of the late Nineteenth and early Twentieth Centuries, and the resulting rush out of the rural areas, came the formation of ghettos. Ethnic groups lived in more and more isolation in certain neighborhoods of cities, and it is said that in some quarters there were white people who had never seen a black face to face. Their information came from the media, such as magazines and books. Caricatures and prejudicial portrayals were widespread and showed a negative and discriminatory picture of the blacks. For that reason, prettied-up black children, fat mammies with thick red lips and lazy scoundrels reproduced not only on quilts but on all imaginable domestic objects for decades. Only in the mid-Twentieth Century did this degrading characterization change to any great degree. The quilts of the time dealt sensibly with the experiences of the blacks in that they included an awareness of African art and culture.[166]

Hawaiian Quilts

Although the Hawaiian Islands in the North Pacific Ocean have been an American territory only since 1893 and became the 49th state of the union in 1954, there were quilts there since the first half of the Nineteenth Century. Their existence can be attributed to the influence of English and Americans. There has to date been no agreement as to when the Polynesians' first contact with Europeans, so important to the later development of quilt making, took place.

It is said that Captain Cook discovered Hawaii in 1778, though Spaniards had sailed to the islands by 1555. Under King Kamehameha I the inhabited larger islands were united into one kingdom. Textile handicrafts are known to have existed there since 1809. A document of 1817 exists that reports on the cotton clothing of a member of the ruling class and several women.[167] This is important insofar as the Polynesians until then knew only tapa, a "cloth" made of compacted mulberry tree bark, of which they made clothing. Because tapa was not washable, the introduction of American textiles was most welcome. On April 3, 1820, a ship with American missionaries and their wives landed on the coast of Hawaii. Four feminine members of the royal family visited the strange women on board their ship. They hoped the American women could help them make stylish clothes. They brought along the cotton cloth to be used, which they had bought from trading ships that stopped at Hawaii on the Pacific route.[168] During this meeting the women, who were not able to help with the sewing of clothes, were busy making patchwork.[169] The diaries of the missionaries tell in great detail of the lives of the Polynesians on Hawaii, but they do not even mention the making of quilts. Although applique quilts believed to date back to 1840 have been preserved at the Honolulu Academy of Arts,[170] the early history of Hawaii's quilt tradition is obscure.

Hawaiian applique quilts were normally made of cotton cloth bought specifically for the planned project. White, or more rarely another light color, was chosen for the background. To this was applied an ornamental pattern cut out of folded cloth of a contrasting color. This technique, according to several researchers,[171] was introduced in Hawaii only around 1860 by the Pennsylvania Dutch, when they set up mission schools there in which needlework was taught. The Pennsylvania Dutch liked to use not only the most varied

99 Applique quilt with red eagles and maple leaves, circa 1870. Atef-Schreiterer Collection, Berlin, West Germany.

flower motifs but particularly oak-leaf or maple-leaf patterns amazingly similar to the breadfruit tree-leaf patterns of traditional Hawaiian quilts (#99). Elsewhere it is said that the missionaries had already introduced the technique of paper cutting, since cutting patterns with scissors was a very popular and highly payed art on the mainland. Therefore the Polynesian women, quite on their own, must have adapted this technique to the textile formation of their quilts.[172] They were also inspired by the flora of their homeland. Flowers and trees were normally portrayed in stylized form, in which three stages of their development, such as bud, blossom and fruit, were shown (#100). The portrayal of animals on quilts was believed to bring bad luck. Regardless of what course the development of Hawaiian quilt styles followed, these creations stand out through their particular decorativity and independence. The patterns were always invented anew and no copying was permitted, since they were regarded as the property of the originator. Their naming was just as individual and full of symbolism.

100 Hawaiian quilt, red applique on white background, 20th Century, 211 x 191. American Museum in Britain, Claverton Manor, Bath, UK.

The name accompanied the quilt as long as it existed. As a rule, the patterns were stressed by quilting their contours. The lines of quilting extended the edges of the motif over all the free space of the quilt like an echo. Along with quilts having general floral patterns, there were those that referred to the royal family in motifs and colors. The crown, the queen's tortoiseshell comb or feather fan, were sewn on quilts as ornaments in red and yellow (representing gold).[173]

Flag quilts have a very special significance for the Polynesian inhabitants of the former Kingdom of Hawaii (#101). King Kamehameha I visited Great Britain at the beginning of the Nineteenth Century and returned to his realm so impressed that he immediately had a palace built and assumed a crown and other symbols such as were used at the English court. The Union Jack was also taken as the national flag and was meant to document the friendship with the island kingdom of Great Britain. Its seven stripes represented the seven main islands under the direct rule of King Kamehameha I. Only in 1845 did the Island of Kauai, which until

101 Flag quilt, Hawaiian, circa 1893, 203 x 178. American
Museum in Britain, Claverton Manor, Bath, UK.

then had been only tributary, become a full-fledged part of the
kingdom and give the flag an eighth stripe.

The climatic conditions of Hawaii are naturally poor for the
preservation of textiles, and it is almost impossible to find quilts
from the time before 1875. All known surviving flag quilts are from
the latter half of the Nineteenth Century and thus have eight stripes
in their motifs. The most commonly used layout was the arrangement
of four flags around a center with crown, coat of arms or other
symbols of rule in red, white and blue. Less frequently used
variations also exist. Since the union with the United States in 1893
and the associated fall of Queen Liliuokalani, it was forbidden to
hoist up the old Hawaiian national flag. "My Beloved Flag" was
used more often as a quilt motif then, for very patriotic reasons. Most
of the native familes who possess quilts preserve at least one flag quilt
as a family treasure, which is passed on from generation to
generation without ever being seen by any outsider. It is believed that
the spirit of the person who sewed the quilt lives on in it, and many

women presumably preserved the instruction for making their quilt, which was supposed to be burned at their death.[175]

Hawaiian quilts were collected in museums very early and valued as unique cultural-historical documents. Within the population they were always regarded as treasures symbolizing the privilege and status of the higher classes. They are impressive evidence that applique and patchwork techniques could be raised to a high artistic level not only via the Euro-American cultural background. The Polynesians were capable of deliberate expression of their esthetic sensitivity and to contribute at least an equivalent to the Euro-American quilt tradition.

Today the tradition of Hawaiian quilts is maintained only by professional seamstresses. They sew quilts chiefly to sell to tourists. The mythos of the old applique quilts thus seems to have died out.

American Quilts of the Early 20th Century

In America after the turn of the century, the production of patchwork quilts remained a popular activity, especially in rural areas. The place as a status symbol, as possessed by the splendid applique quilts and later the challenging crazy quilts, faded away with the growing popularity for simple patchwork quilts. Their appearance was characterized by the dark, unicoloured cotton prints popular at the beginning of the century, called "Shaker gray" (#102).[175]

Traditional patchwork patterns, as well as new patchwork block designs, were published in magazines such as "Woman's Home Companion" or "The Modern Priscilla", which rapidly spread their popularity throughout North America. Developments in the world of art at that time, such as was expressed in Art Deco, is reflected in the motifs of new patchwork patterns. In the period from 1925 to 1940, known as the "Depression Era", a very typical patchwork style developed, which can be recognized both in the particular types of cloth used and in the patchwork itself. Most of the quilts that have survived to this day come from this time of worldwide economic crisis, in which the practical as well as the esthetic aspects of quilts took on a new importance.

The cotton prints of the second quarter of the century were usually very colorful. Orange, yellow and other glowing colors dominated. Commercial interests dictated the possibilities, and low-cost production expressed itself clearly in the appearance of the fabrics. Missing details meant less production time to be spent engraving the copper drums; the simplicity of the motifs did not require any exact setting of the machines. So flowers, for example, were stylized, rather than time and trouble being put into the characterization of specific types. White borders around printed motifs indicate that even in the planning stages the imprecision of the printing machines were planned on.[176] The colorful aspect was very obviously meant to make up for this deficiency, for by then there were many cheap dyes available. On the other hand, printing placard-like and stylized motifs on cloth was fashionable at that time.

102 Scrap quilt top, with detail, beginning of the 20th Century, 222 x 190. Privately owned by Rosa Dames, Berlin, West Germany.

Detail of #102.

Since the last quarter of the Nineteenth Century, white, brown and other solid-color cotton cloth had been made into packing material, the so-called "feed sacks". Grain, flour, sugar and other commodities were stored and sold in them. They often gave good service as material for the backs of quilts. The printed names of the firms, often still visible, now and then offer useful hints of the time and place of origin of a quilt. Since the Thirties, at least, colorfully printed feed sacks were also used for patchwork. In the time of the worldwide economic crisis people got into the habit of making something useful of all usable materials. So the patterned cotton sacks were opened up, washed and ironed, then to be used anew. Making patchwork quilts of them was obvious, but in time of need everything else, even

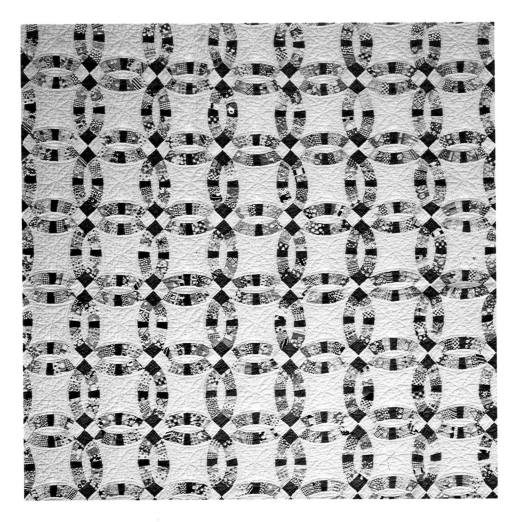

103 Patchwork quilt, "Double Wedding Ring", circa 1930, 200 x 180. Folk Art Gallery, Hamburg, West Germany.

164

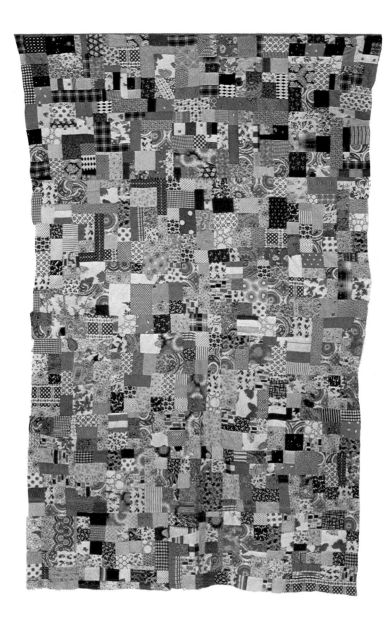

104 Scrap quilt top, with detail, circa 1930, 232 x 180. Privately owned by Rosa Dames, Berlin, West Germany.

children's underwear, was made out of this cloth. In a "Textile Bag Manufacturer's Booklet", as well as in magazines, hints were offered for the removal of the printing and firm emblems. Despite that, a woman recalled spending her whole childhood in "Pillsbury's Best" underwear, since "Pillsbury's Best" did not bleach out.[177] A virtue was made of necessity when the "Scrap Quilts", very popular at that time, were made of as many different cloths as possible (# 104). Packages of cloth scraps, which could be bought for 25 cents, added to

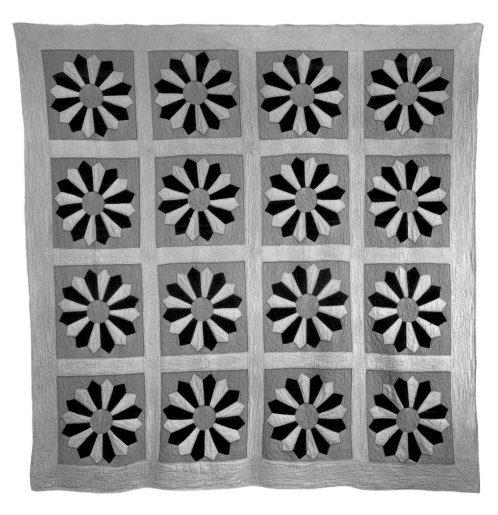

105 Aster quilt, similar to the Dresden Plate pattern, in the typical colors of the 1920-30 era. Folk Art Gallery, Hamburg, West Germany.

the variety of fabrics for such projects. In this situation patchwork blocks gained new honors, with their patterns assembled from the basic elements of square and triangle. For patchwork patterns with matched colors, one naturally needed larger quantities of one and the same cloth. To that purpose sacks with the desired patterns were traded with friends and neighbors, sacks were reserved at stores, or empty sacks were bought from bakers. It is very hard to determine in hindsight whether patchwork quilts of this era were made of feed-sack fabrics or newly purchased cotton prints if no regular stitching holes of the earlier sack seams or at least parts of a logo can be found.[178]

Along with printed fabrics, solid colors in pastel shades were especially typical of the Twenties and Thirties (# 107). A very distinct pale and cold greenish-gray, as well as a faded pinkish-purple red

106 Patchwork quilt, "Cornucopia", circa 1920-30. Folk Art Gallery, Hamburg, West Germany.

could almost symbolize this era. Traditional and new applique motifs, as well as original quilt patterns, were applied in these colors to white backgrounds. Comparison with late Nineteenth-Century work shows the different effect very drastically. The distribution of motifs in magazines included exact cutting patterns and detailed descriptions, the significance of which in this context should not be underrated. Whole kits, containing the needed materials as well as instructions, could be bought. The same was good for traditional patchwork patterns, including the "Dresden Plate" and "Aster" variations (#105),[179] the hexagonal "Grandmother's Flower Garden", composites[180] and fan patterns[181] (#106) which enjoyed the greatest popularity. As a relatively new patchwork pattern, the "Double Wedding Ring",[182] (#103) was typical of this period. Unlike the mostly stylized forms of flower motifs in Nineteenth-Century

107 Tulip applique quilt, 1910-20, 250 x 205. Folk Art Gallery, Hamburg, West Germany.

appliques as well as the repeated flowers on printed fabrics of the early Twentieth Century, clearly recognizable types of flowers such as iris, roses and water lilies now came to the fore. An important new development was the making of children's quilts, which were decorated with the "Sunbonnet Babies", "Sunbonnet Sue" and "Overall Sam" figures of Bertha L. Corbett[183] and naive animal designs. Such detailed and totally unified patchwork quilts, as we find them in the decades between the World Wars, would have been unthinkable without the instructions in the magazines. Local elements of style had scarcely any chance of surviving beside them.

Since the beginning of the Twentieth Century, interest in patchwork quilts has declined steadily, for understandable reasons. The work of women was needed in more important places, and there was no more time to do time-consuming handicrafts, though their usefulness was evident and their preparation was a creative and social pastime.

On the Way to Quilt Art

The heights of the American patchwork quilt tradition are doubtless in the latter half of the Nineteenth Century and the Twenties and Thirties of our century. As a creative art, they held up a mirror to their times. The life situations of the people who created them, the regional, religious and ethnic connections, standards and fashions found expression in these quilts. Typical characteristics of their creation, marked by free discussion of the trends of the times, indicate their origin and make them cultural-historical documents. "American folk art is not an inept form of high art. It lives in its own world and reacts to its own surroundings. It was created by dilettantes who worked for their own satisfaction and the praise of their families and neighbors."[184]

On the one hand the vast amount of movement within the American people, as well as the spread of the media, contributed to the growing popularity of patchwork quilts. On the other hand, thereby traditionally developed forms of creation were released from their background and became familiar and useful to everyone. The decorative rediscovery of the past, that cannot really be revived in terms of its impetus and significance, led not to real innovation, but only to exact repetition of patterns, forms and colors.

Traditional patchwork and quilting still enjoy much popularity today, especially in the rural regions of America. But very few women still practice it as a tradition that was handed down from grandmothers to daughters and granddaughters.[185] The great majority of them are those who learn these textile techniques from books and in courses as a spare-time activity. In the cities there are specialty shops that offer fabrics, interlinings, thread, instructions, quilt patterns— in short, all that is needed. Quilting clubs and mail-order firms are there to meet the needs of interested people. The exact number of active so-called quilt makers in America is not known, but is estimated to be about seven million. There are six regularly appearing periodicals on the subject, the most popular of which, the "Quilter's Newsletter Magazine" alone, has 70,000 subscribers. There are also many catalogs and countless books about patchwork

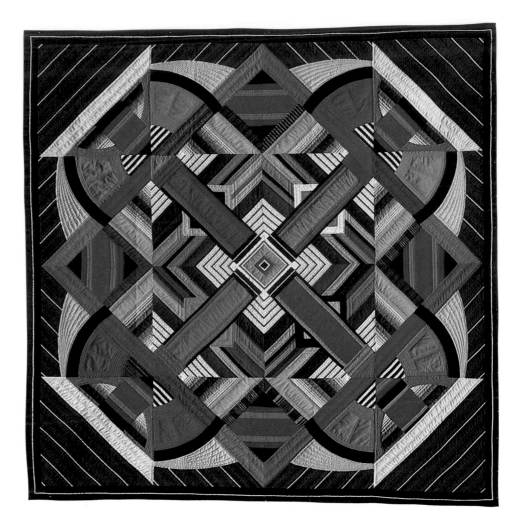

108 Nancy Crow: "Bittersweet", 1982, machine-sewn and hand-quilted, 241 x 241. Owned by its creator.

and quilting. Active quilt makers have organized almost six hundred quilt clubs. Hundreds of "Historical Societies" and museums possess great collections of quilts, quilt displays are organized by churches, artistic groups, welfare societies and other organizations and attract many spectators.[186] Similar tendencies, though much more modest in numbers, are seen in the European countries, particularly England.[187] Patchwork and quilting have become a popular hobby that is not going to thwart creativity because of any lack of material or inspiration. Quite the opposite, one could sometimes get the impression that the overflow leaves too little room to work up the courage for individual creativity.

170

109 Michael James: "Interweave III, 1982, machine-sewn and quilted, 180 x 180. Owned by its creator.

In consequence, one sees now and then an attempt to utilize old techniques to find new means of modern interpretation. What is original becomes an independent new creation, not afraid of experimentation, self-sufficient, and no longer needing to live up to the demands of utility. The fulness of creative potential lies in breaking loose from geometry, in free variations of colors, forms, materials and creative techniques. Only along this path could the patchwork quilt again become a mirror of the present time that provided its inspiration. The quilt developed in this sense in America in the Seventies, and since then has developed increasingly in Europe, into an exciting part of textile art.

171

110 Terrie Hancock Mangat, "Lightning Runner", 1984, patchwork and applique, hand-quilted, 208 x 165.

111 David Hornung, "The Nile", 1984, patchwork, hand-quilted, 211 x 127.

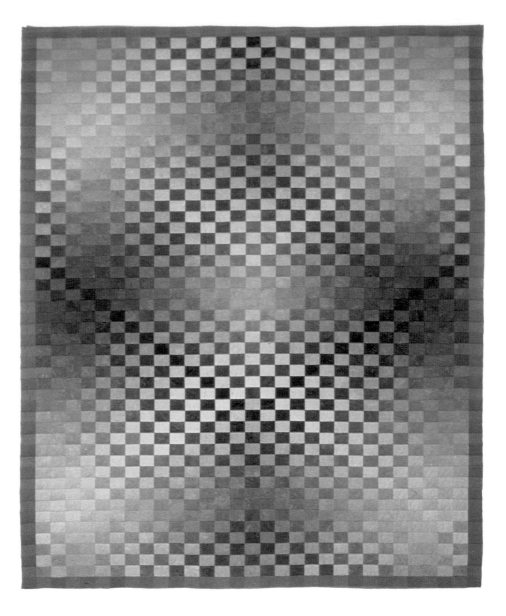

112 Jan Myers, "Galaxial Four Patch", 1984, patchwork, hand-quilted, 188 x 160.

The first exhibition of modern quilts took place in the New York Museum of Contemporary Crafts in 1976. Every one of them presented new thematic or technical aspects and helped to illustrate the manifold possibilities of creative trends. "This official valuation legitimized the modern quilt and lifted it above the great mass of conventional quilts anchored in the old traditions. The modern quilt gives evidence to the self-awareness of its creators, who want to win a reputation for themselves and official recognition for their work."[188]

For two highly regarded exhibitions, Charlotte Robinson ("The Artist and the Quilt", 1982)[189] and Ludy Strauss (Artist's Quilts", 1981)[190] have been competing since the mid-Seventies to further the cooperation of artists and quilt makers. This has had very fruitful effects in both directions, as it could be learned from the completed exhibitions, and yet the whole thing must be regarded as an experiment. Such publicity as threatened to repress their capability in terms of handicraft could have hurt the quilt artists involved.

How independent and creative they can be, on the other hand, is chown by the regular biennial "Quilt National" exhibitions held since 1979 in Athens, Ohio. A jury of experts judges the array of

113 Pauline Burbidge, "Finn", 1983, patchwork, quilted, 241 x 236.

examples, the niveau of which rises from year to year. At first a domain of Americans above all, it has seen increasing competition from European quilt artists in the last few years. Similar exhibitions also take place in England, France, Germany and Switzerland. Whereas Nancy Crow won an art award, previously reserved for paintings, in America in 1983 with her quilt, "Interlacings I", the recognition of modern quilts has come hard in Europe. Too often the judges are too wrapped up in old traditional concepts to be able to be objective. In the end it is a matter of time until quilt makers gain the recognition due them in the world of international textile art. On this path too, the Americans are leading the way. Modern quilts are often seen in banks, hotel foyers and public halls, and are treasured by museums and collectors.

Significant for the self-awareness of quilt makers are the subtitles given to past "Quilt National" exhibitions. In 1983 it was "New Directions for an American Tradition", in 1985 "The State of an Art".[191] The idea could scarcely be formulated more deliberately and convincingly. Influenced by the traditions of its own discipline as well as by historical and contemporary trends in creative art in general, the formative power of a quilt maker is nevertheless shaped most of all by the awareness of being a lone traveler of unexplored territory.[192]

Modern quilts make it clear that the technical and artistic boundaries of the medium are very broad. The pattern was set, though, with but few exceptions, by the traditional "bed-cover format", sometimes a bit bigger, sometimes smaller. Within this freely chosen frame, the quilt makers seek out the textile qualities and structural particulars of their theme. Fabrics purchased or dyed at home, velvet as well as silk, solid-colored as well as patterned cotton are customary materials; plastic and paper serve for experimenting. Painting, spraying, printing and photographic technology further the creative possibilities. The main themes of most quilt makers have remained forms and colors. Their composition can be as subtle and sensitive as in the case of Michael James (# 109) or Pam Studstill, or as loud and direct as with Nancy Crow (# 108) or Françoise Barnes. Motifs with strong tendencies to traditional patchwork can have a startlingly modern effect under certain conditions, while hitherto unheard-of formative concepts scarcely go beyond familiar impressions. A love for textile materials and their structures can be just as powerful a theme as colorful realistic detail in formal composition. The freedom to design a patchwork quilt seems to have become endless, and many have made use of it. The best-known quilt makers, in addition to those already named, are Ivonne Porcella, Terrie Hancock Mangat (# 110), Jan Myers (# 112), David Hornung (# 111) and many others who have already found their individual styles

111 Dorle Stern-Straeter, "Oasis", 1984, patchwork, hand-quilted, 160 x 160.

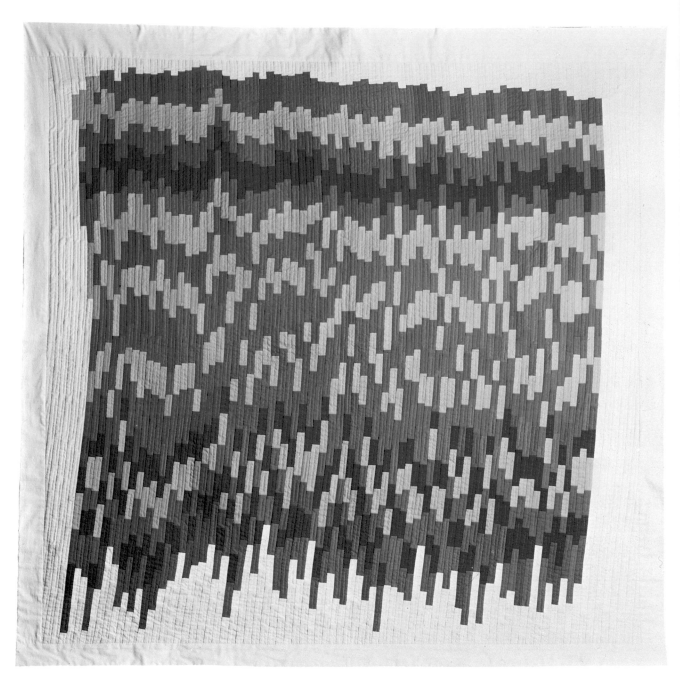

115 Rosa Dames, "Blue Runs Away", 1985, patchwork, hand-quilted, 218 x 218.

over the years and work very successfully to develop them further. Pauline Burbridge can be named as an outstanding English quilt artist (# 113). Her three-dimensional illusions in patchwork technique have already won her many significant honors and awards. But Michele Walker and Lucy Wallis are also significant artists from Great Britain, who have made their names with innovative quilts. In Germany, Dorle Stern-Straeter (#114), Inge Hueber and Rosa Dames (# 115) belong among the avant-garde of modern patchwork quilting and have gained international recognition.

Yet any list of names in this context must remain incomplete and thereby perhaps also unjust. Regardless of where in the world quilts originate—made by a Nineteenth-Century pioneer woman, an Indian farm wife or a Twentieth-Century quilt maker, a quilt remains an object that can be appreciated in all its dimensions only by one's own observation, by a direct confrontation between object and observer. More than just a picture and more than just a quilt, it involves all the senses, which can take place only partially in a photo or a description.

Collecting and Caring for Patchwork Quilts

There are many possible ways to obtain an antique or modern patchwork quilt. In addition to the obvious visit to a gallery, auction or antique shop, one can sometimes find a quilt, as it were, beside the road or through chance contact. In this respect, there are no limits to the chances. But before one uses one's chances, one should get thorough information, see and feel carefully. Often enough a new quilt is offered for sale as an old one, and it needs a trained eye to be able to judge the seller's claims by one's own examination and experience. The previous descriptions of fabrics, processes and work techniques can be useful in avoiding misjudgments and disappointments from the start. In spite of that, expressed doubt and healthy mistrust are always the best advisors in buying a quilt or patchwork top.

With growing interest from collectors, museums and commercial firms, the prices of antique quilts are also increasing rapidly. The condition, age and originality of a design and the color composition as well as the technical finishing are decisive in determining the price. On the other hand, the taste of the time plays a role that is not to be underrated. In past years Amish quilts were considered the "non plus ultra" by quilt fanciers, and that had a natural effect on prices. Scrap quilts of the Twenties and Thirties, though, could be had comparatively cheaply. But fashions change quickly, and it doesn't do to set concrete prices—tomorrow everything can be different. In any case, one must be ready to pay four-figure prices. In the end, quilts also have a subjective price for the interested person. The piece is only worth to him what he is ready to pay for it. An outsider's criticism of a supposedly excessive price is to a great extent equally subjective, if in a different way.

Modern quilts made by living quilt artists have prices similar, for example, to the paintings of present-day artists. The price is determined by artistic and technical quality as well as the artist's degree of renown. A modern bedquilt with a traditional pattern is realistically priced, according to its size, at one to two thousand dollars.[193]

Once one possesses an antique quilt, one should give serious thought to its care, preservation and presentation, in order to maintain its material and aesthetic worth as long as possible. An antique quilt, whether of cotton, silk or wool, should certainly not be washed or dry-cleaned. A layman will scarcely be in a position to judge whether in a special case a quilt can be washed or chemically cleaned. Before one ruins a good and valuable piece, one should give it a careful brushing with a very soft brush and air it regularly. As a rule, most people are only disturbed by the ugly brown mildew stains on the cloth. Unfortunately, nothing will remove these, no matter how sharp or secretive. Perhaps one should learn to accept them with the understanding that age always leaves its traces, on textiles as well as or on us ourselves. Other objects also acquire a patina that, often enough, emphasizes their value in a purely external way. Unfortunately, mildew speaks not only for age, but also for ill-treatment. It is usually caused by too much moisture in the air, when condensation water can be deposited on the cloth. For this reason, one should never store quilts in plastic bags.

Light is an equally great enemy of antique textiles. Ultra-violet rays destroy dyes and pigments and hasten the deterioration of the fibers. The colors fade and the weave begins to come apart. So when one hangs up an old quilt, one should never let direct sunlight strike it. Even modern textiles that are dyed with lightfast chemical colors would not last long under such extreme conditions and would lose their color.

The optimal conditions for storing old quilts, namely spread out flat and protected from dust, can be attained only in museums. When one must store them folded up, the following method is suggested. The quilt should be spread out on a clean surface and covered with tissue paper. During careful folding, the folds should be padded with crumpled tissue paper, so that no sharp folds occur in the cloth. The cloth would deteriorate most easily at such bends. The folded quilt should be housed in a sufficiently large carton or a drawer. The container must be lined with tissue paper or washed cotton cloth, so that the quilt does not come into contact with acid-containing wood or cardboard. A quilt covered with tissue paper can just as well be rolled loosely around a bamboo pole and then covered with a washed cotton cloth. Which method is more suitable depends on the available space.

There are two good ways to hang a quilt. A strip of (velcro or) adhesive tape (about 4cm wide) can be sewn by machine onto a cotton strip at least one centimeter wide. This can then be tacked by hand onto the upper edge of the back of the quilt. One should be sure to attach all three layers of cloth carefully, so as to divide the stress better. The opposite side of the adhesive tape should be attached to a piece of wood a little shorter than the width of the quilt. After one has attached the tape, one hangs up the quilt via the wood. If the quilt pattern allows, it is recommended to hang it by a different side every few months, as the cloth might otherwise tear from constant stress. The effectiveness of the adhesive must also be checked regularly.

It is more protective to build a wooden frame of the right size and cover it with washed cotton cloth. The quilt is then tacked to this cloth with parallel zigzag stitching and thus supported. One should never hang the quilt up by itself, as it would scarcely survive this stress over a long time. The way of hanging just described is especially suited to very old and worn quilts.[194]

Modern quilts can usually be dry-cleaned, or washed if they are made of cotton. Otherwise, though, one should not be any less careful with them than with their antique brethren.

Footnotes

1. Averil Colby, Quilting, London, 1972, reprinted 1983, p. 8.
2. Mary Morgan and Dee Mosteller, Trapunto, New York, 1977, p. 7.
3. Lenice Ingram Bacon, American Patchwork Quilts, New York, 1973, p. 50.
4. Morgan & Mosteller, op. cit., pp. 10-11.
5. Colby, op. cit., pp. 91ff.
6. Interesting information can be found in Tandy Hersh, 18th Century Quilted Silk Petticoats Worn in America, in: Uncoverings, Vol. 5, 1984, pp. 83-98.
7. Sally Garoutte, Marseille Quilts and Their Woven Offspring, in: Uncoverings, Vol. 3, 1982, pp. 115-134.
8. Averil Colby, Patchwork, London, 1958, reprinted 1983, pp. 86-87.
9. Barbara von Roemer, Patchwork und Quilts, Stuttgart, 1982, pp. 14-15.
10. Catalog of the "Gold of the Scythians" exposition, Munich, West Germany, 1984, pp. 178-185, 198.
11. Averil Colby, Patchwork, London, 1958 (1983), p. 21, #109.
12. Annegret Haake, lecture on an exposition, "Patchwork, Quilts, Javan Batik", in Kronberg/Taunus, West Germany, December 11, 1985.
13. Comment by Dr. Hartmut Wallravens, Hamburg, West Germany; source: Morohashi, T.: Dai Kan-Wa Jiten, No. 22679444, in which the source is given as the Buddhist work Fo ma chih tu lun (no date).
14. Torvald Faigre, Tents—Architecture of the Nomads, London, 1979, pp. 12-17.
15. H. R. Dickson, The Arab of the Desert, Bedawin Life in Kuwait and Saudi Arabia, London, 1949, pp. 66-75.
16. T. Faigre, op. cit., pp. 65-70.
17. M. Breitenbach, Im Land der Wilden Reiter, Frankfurt, West Germany, 1981; Dorit Berger, Kirghisische Yurten, in: Deutsches Textilforum 1/1982, p. 19.
18. Peter Jaeckel, Anmerkungen zur Turkenbeute, in: Katalog Türkische Kunst und Kultur aus osmanischer Zeit, Vol. 2, Recklinghausen, West Germany, 1985, pp. 351-353.
19. Die Türkenbeute—Bildheft des Badischen Landesmuseums, Karlsruhe, West Germany, 1970; Agnes Geijer, Oriental Textiles in Sweden, Copenhagen, 1951, p. 71.
20. Harriet Bridgeman and Elizabeth Drury (Eds.), Geschichte der Textilkunst, Ravensburg, 1978, p. 282, Plate 100
21. The Bible, translated by Martin Luther, Württembergische Bibelanstalt, Stuttgart, 1962, Exodus 25:4 & 26:1.
22. The Bible, op. cit., Ezekiel 27:7.
23. Picture Bible from the Pantheon, Roman School, 12th Century, Vatican Library (MS Vat. Lat. 72958, c. 60 v.), The Vatican.
24. Kurt Zipper, Ägyptische Zeltteppiche, in: Kunst und Antiquitäten, III/1978, pp. 10-12.
25. For example, in the Ethnographic Museum of Berlin, West Germany and the Museum of Mankind, London.
26. F. E. Forbes, Dahomey and the Dahomans, being the Journals of two Missions to the King of Dahomey and Residence of his Capital in the Years 1849 and 1850, 2 vol., London, 1851.
27. Monni Adams, Fon Appliqued Cloths, in: African Art, UCLA, Vol. 13, No. 2, February 1980, pp. 28-41.
28. R. Gardi, Unter Afrikanischen Handwerkern, Bern, CH, 1969, pp. 224-229.
29. M. Adams, op. cit., p. 34.
30. Jill Salmons, Funary Shrine Cloths of the Annang Ibibio, South East Nigeria, Ed. Dale Indiens & K. G. Ponting, Bath, GB, 1980, pp. 120-139.

31. Vickie C. Elson, Dowries from Kutch, Exhibition Catalog, Museum of Cultural History, Los Angeles, 1975.
32. Eberhard Fischer, Rural Craftsmen and Their Work, National Institute of Design, Ahmedabad, 1970, pp. 183ff.
33. John Irwin and Margaret Hall, Historical Textiles of India at the Calico Museum, Ahmedabad, 1973, p. 118.
34. Bunting, Sindhi Tombs and Textiles—The Persistance of Pattern, pp. 63-64. Suggestion of Mrs. Eder, Stuttgart, West Germany.
35. Irwin & Hall, op. cit., p. 85.
36. R. Christoffel, Sind Korak wirklich Korak?, in: Schweizerische Arbeitslehrerinnen Zeitung 3/1982. Suggestion of Mr. Adolf Siegrist, Basel, CH.
37. N. Kaplan and S. Ivanov (Eds.), In The Land of Reindeer, Leningrad, USSR, 1974, pp. 7-8.
38. Paul and Elaine Lewis, Völker im Goldenen Dreieck, Stuttgart, West Germany, 1984, p. 11.
39. Basic are: P. & E. Lewis, op. cit., and Lauri Linch and Alice Schmude, Hmong needle Treasures, in: Quilters Newsletter Magazine, October 1984, pp. 18-22.
40. Basic are: Textiles of Japan III, Okinawan, Ainu and Foreign Designs, compiled by the Japan Textile Colour Center, London, 1980, pp. 19-23.
41. Seiroku Noma, Japanese Costume and Textile Arts, New York-Tokyo, 1974, p. 157.
42. Seiroku Noma, op. cit., pp. 116ff.
43. Venice Lamb, West African Weaving, London, 1980, pp. 14-15.
44. Karl Martin, Reisen in die Molukken, Leiden, 1984, Plate XVIII; Jose/ Casal, The People and Art of Philippines, Los Angeles, 1981, pp. 142-143.
45. Heide Nixdorff, Europäische Volkstrachten, Vol. 1, Czechoslovakia, Berlin, West Germany, 1977, pp. 154-157.
46. Günther Hartmann, Molakana—Volkskunst der Cuna, Panama, Berlin, West Germany, 1980.
47. Sally and Richard Price, Afro-American Arts of the Surinam Rain Forest, Los Angeles, 1980, p. 47, Personal Adornment.
48. Wedding gown in patchwork technique, made of ottoman and satin, in August, 1969, for Her Royal Highness Madame la Duchesse d'Orleans, under contract by Yves Saint Laurent. Exhibition Catalog, Metropolitan Museum of Art (Publ.), New York-Berlin, 1984, #15, No. 79.
49. Gerhard Schweizer, Die Derwische, Salzburg, A, 1980, p. 57.
50. Margit Reichelt Jordan, Patchwork und Applikationen, Munich, 1982, p. 38; Pamela Clabburn, Patchwork, Shire Album 101, Aylesbury, 1983, p. 23.
51. J. Dupuis, Journal of a Residence in Ashantee, London, GB, 1924 (reprinted 1966).
52. Venice Lamb, West African Weaving, London, 1980, pp. 145-146.
53. Heinrich Barth, Reisen und Entdeckungen in Nordund Central-Afrika in den Jahren 1849 bis 1855, published 1857 & 1858, State Archives, Hamburg, West Germany.
54. GEO-Magazin, 26. 8. 1985, Eine Reise nach Afrika, pp. 9ff; Uwe George (mainly pp. 38-39).
55. Annegret Haake, Javanische Batik, Hannover, 1984, p. 61, as well as a lecture at an exhibition: "Patchwork, Quilts, Javan Batik", on Dec. 11, 1985, in Kronberg/Taunus, West Germany, plus the following references: Mattiebelle Gittinger, Splendid Symbols—Textiles and Tradition in Indonesia, Washington, 1979, p. 123, #84-85; Mary Hunt Kahlenberg, Textile Traditions of Indonesia, Los Angeles, 1977, p. 61; Inger McCabe Elliot, Tambal—Patchwork—Batik, New York, 1984.
56. Victoria & Albert Museum, London: Notes on Patchwork, Her Majesty's Stationery Office, 1949. This small volume was very obviously a source for many authors who have written about patchwork.

57. Harriet Bridgeman and Elizabeth Drury (Eds.), Geschichte der Textilkunst, Ravensburg, West Germany, 1978, p. 186.

58. Lenice Ingram Bacon, American Patchwork Quilts, New York, 1973, p. 31, for example.

59. Bridgeman & Drury, pp. 132-133; Annarosa Garzelli, Il ricamo nella attivita artistica di Pollaiuolo, Botticelli, Bartolo di Giovanni, Florence, 1973.

60. Bridgeman & Drury, pp. 197-198.

61. Bacon, p. 44.

62. Bridgeman & Drury, pp. 233-234.

63. Erich Meyer Heisig, Weberei, Nadelwerk, Zeugdruck, Munich, 1956, pp. 59ff; R. Jaques, Deutsche Textilkunst, 1953, pp. 169-171.

64. Mechthild Scholten-Neess, Ein Hungertuch aus Geldern, in: Geldricher Heimatkalender, 1970, pp. 126ff.

65. Averil Colby, Patchwork, London, 1958, reprinted 1983, pp. 96ff.

66. Fustian (Barchent) is a fabric with linen warp and cotton weft. It has the character of coarse cotton flannel.

67. Hazel Clark, Textile Printing, Aylesbury, 1985; Shire Album 135, pp. 6ff.

68. Colby, Patchwork, p. 103.

69. Marguerite Ickis, Quilt Making, New York, 1949, pp. 258-259.

70. John Smith, Generall History of Virginia, London, 1624.

71. Basic are particularly Charlotte Lutkins, Die Gründung des englischen Kolonialreiches in Nordamerika, in: Ciba-Rundschau 39-40, July-August 1939, pp. 1435-1440 and Barbara Tuchmann, Die Torheit der Regierenden, Chapter 4: Die Briten verlieren Amerika, Frankfurt, 1984, pp. 158-259.

72. Averil Colby, Patchwork, London, 1958, p. 29; Hazel Clark, Textile Printing, Aylesbury, 1985.

73. Averil Colby's book about patchwork is to date the most inclusive in terms of information on the history of English patchwork. The detailed explanations are very readable, but could be given here only in very reduced form.

74. Marguerite Ickis, Quilt Making, New York, 1949, p. 259.

75. The "Navigation Acts" of 1651, 1660, 1663 and 1673 were meant to keep the colonies economically dependent on England. All trade with the colonies could be carried out only on English ships. All textile production in the colonies was forbidden. "Sugar, tobacco, cotton, indigo, ginger, yellow and other coloring wood that are grown or produced in our Asian, African or American colonies, may be shipped from these colonies only to England, Ireland or other possessions of His Majesty."

76. Jonathan Holstein, The Pieced Quilt, Boston, 1973, p. 26.

77. Charlotte Lütkens, Die Textilgewerbe in der Kolonialzeit, in: Ciba-Rundschau 39-40, July-August 1939, pp. 1442-1447; Petra Mattern-Pabel, Patchwork-Quilt, Hannover, 1981, pp. 22-23.

78. Hazel Clark, Textile Printing, Aylesbury, 1985, pp. 17ff (Shire Album 135).

79. Charlotte Lütkens, Anfänge der nordamerikanischen Baumwollindustrie, in: Ciba-Rundschau 39-40, July-August 1939, pp. 1448-1452.

80. Carleton S. Safford and Robert Bishop, America's Quilts and Coverlets, New York, 1980, p. 29.

81. Barbara Brackman, Dating Old Quilts, part 4, in: Quilters Newsletter Magazine, January 1985, p. 25.

82. Basic are: Charlotte Lütkens, Anfänge der nordamerikanischen Baumwoll-industrie, in: Ciba-Rundschau 39-40, july-August 1939, pp. 1448-1452 and Die Entkörnungsmaschine von Eli Whitney, in Ciba-Rundschau 39-40, july-August 1939; Jonathan Holstein, The Pieced Quilt, Boston, 1973, pp. 29ff; Barbara Brackman, Dating Old Quilts, Parts 1 & 5, in: Quilters Newsletter Magazine, September 1984 and February 1985.

83. James M. Liles, Dyes in American Quilts Before 1930, in: Uncoverings 5, Mill Valley CA, 1985.

84. Tandy Hersh, Some Aspects of an 1809 Quilt, in: Uncoverings, Vol. 3, 1982, p. 4.

85. Jean Taylor Federico, White Work Classification System, in: Uncoverings, Vol. 1, 1980, p. 68.

86. Probably no patchwork or applique quilts were made in North America before 1750. There were imported quilts and the aforementioned wholecloth quilts. See also: Sally Garoutte, Early Colonial Quilts in a Bedding Context, in: Uncoverings, Vol. 1, 1980, pp. 18ff, and Florence Peto, New York Quilts, in: New York History, Vol. 30, No. 3, July 1949.

87. The so-called Saltonstall Quilt was formerly dated to 1704 and regarded as the oldest surviving American patchwork quilt. It has a geometric pattern of brocade silk and velvet, partially underlaid by a paper inlay (Harvard college Catalog of 1701). Ann Farnam, Curator at Essex Institute, Salem, suggests a late 18thor early 19th-Century date as a result of thorough investigation. See Barbara Brackman, A Chronological Index to Pieced Quilt Patterns, in: Uncoverings, Vol. 4, 1983, p. 102, and Dating Old Quilts, Part 6, in Quilter's Newsletter Magazine, March 1985, p. 23.

88. Jonathan Holstein, The Pieced Quilt, Boston, 1973, p. 27.

89. Tandy Hersh, Some Aspects of an 1809 Quilt, in: Uncoverings, Vol. 3, 1982, p. 11.

90. Ruth Finley, Old Patchwork Quilts, 1929, reprinted 1983, p. 23.

91. Marquerite Ickis, Quilt Making, New York, 1949, pp. 260-262.

92. Der Grosse Brockhaus, Wiesbaden, 1957, Vol. 12, pp. 104ff., and Ruth Finley, Old Patchwork Quilts, Philadelphia, 1929, reprinted 1983.

93. Lenice I. Bacon, American Patchwork Quilts, New York, 1973.

94. Ellen F. Eanes, Nine Related Quilts of Mecklenburg County, 1800-1840, in: Uncoverings, Vol. 3, 1982, pp. 25-42.

95. Lydia Maria Child, The American Frugal Housewife, New York, 1845, p. 1.

96. Lynn A. Bonfield, The Production of Cloth, Clothing and Quilts in 19th New England Homes, in: Uncoverings, Vol. 2, p. 84.

97. Basic was: Barbara Brackman, A Chronological Index to Pieced Quilt Patterns 1775-1825, in: Uncoverings, Vol. 4, 1983, pp. 99ff. There 139 North American patchwork quilts are covered, of which at least fifteen each come from New York, New England and Pennsylvania.

98. Judy Mathieson, Mariner's Compass, in: Uncoverings, Vol. 2, 1981, p. 12.

99. Jinny Beyers, The Quilter's Album of Blocks and Borders, London, 1980, p. 3.

100. For example, Yvonne Khin, The Collectors Dictionary of Quilt Names and Patterns, Washington, 1980, and John L. Oldani, Folklore Archive at Southern Illinois University, Box 43, SIUE, Edwardsville IL 62025.

101. Carrie E. Hall and Rose G. Kretsinger, The Romance of the Patchwork Quilt, Kansas, 1935, p. 79.

102. Hall & Kretsinger, p. 91.

103. The various forms of making patchwork quilts were systematized by Jonathan Holstein in his book, "The Pieced Quilt", Boston, 1973, pp. 17-18.

104. Lenice Ingram Bacon, American Patchwork Quilts, New York, 1973, p. 15.

105. Hall & Kretsinger, p. 65.

106. Hall & Kretsinger, pp. 64, 66; Cuesta Benberry, White Perceptions of Blacks in Quilts and Related Media, in: Uncoverings, Vol. 4, 1983, p. 61.

107. Ruth Finley, Old Patchwork Quilts, Philadelphia, 1929, reprinted 1983, p. 109. 108. Hall & Kretsinger, p. 75.

109. Hall & Kretsinger, p. 119.

110. Ruth Finley, p. 111, and Katy Christopherson, The Political and Campaign Quilt, Lexington, Kentucky 1984. 111. Hall & Kretsinger, p. 116.

112. Frankfurter Allgemeine Zeitung, Oct. 23, 1985, p. 8.

113. John Rice Irwin, A People and Their Quilts, Exton, Pennsylvania, 1983, p. 53.

114. Jonathan Holstein, The Pieced Quilt, Boston, 1973, p. 26.

115. Patsy and Myron Orlofsky, Quilts in America, New York, 1974.

116. This subject is dealt with more thoroughly by Jonathan Holstein, op. cit., pp. 88-89, and Averil Colby, Quilting, London, 1972, reprinted 1983, beginning on page 40.

117. In "Home Needlework Magazine" of 1899 there are advertisements for Payson's indelible ink, for marking linen, silk and cotton. A supplement announces that Payson has been a housekeeping tradition for over 65 years... One can conclude that Payson's had been on the market since circa 1834. See particularly Linda Otto Lipsett, Remember Me, San Francisco, 1985, pp. 16-18.

118. A selection of the most important titles on this subject: Florence Montgomery, Printed Textiles: English and American cottons and Linens 1700-1850, New York, 1970; Patsy and Myron Orlofsky, Quilts in America, New York, 1974; Florence Pettit, America's Printed and Painted Fabrics 1600-1900, New York, 1970; Dena S. Katzenberg, Baltimore Album Quilts, The Baltimore Museum of Art, 1982, pp. 33-37, with a thorough bibliography on the subject of fabrics and of textile printing in the USA; Katherine R. Koob, Documenting Quilts by Their Fabrics, in: Uncoverings, Vol. 2, 1981, pp. 3-9; James M. Liles, Dyes in American Quilts Made Prior to 1930, with special emphasis on cotton and linen, in: Uncoverings, Vol. 5, 1984, pp. 29ff; a good overview is given by Barbara Brackman in six installments in Quilter's Newsletter Magazine, under the title: Dating Old Quilts, September 1984, pp. 24ff, October 1984, pp. 26ff, November-December 1984, pp. 16ff, January 1985, pp. 28ff, February 1985, pp. 22ff, March 1985, pp. 22ff.

119. Kate Greenaway lived from 1846 to 1901 and was a popular author and illustrator of children's books. "Under the Window" of 1879 is one of her most famous books.

120. Florence Pettit refers to the color scheme of Paisley prints as "The Madder-Style", since all the parts of the motifs could be printed with madder and needed only to be treated with stains of varying intensity for the different shades of color. 121. Basic is the literature listed in footnote 119.

122. "Godey's Lady's Book Magazine" was published since the early 1830»s by Sarah J. Hale of New England, and attained by the time of the Civil War a printing of 150,000 copies.

123. Jinny Beyer, The Quilter's Album of Blocks & Borders, London, 1982, Chapter 1, pp. 3ff; Virginia Gunn, Victorian Silk Template Patchwork in American Periodicals 1850-1875, in: Uncoverings, Vol. 4, 1983, pp. 9-25.

124. Jonathan Holstein, The Pieced Quilt, Boston, 1973, pp. 115-116.

125. Sandi Fox, The Log Cabin—An American Quilt on the Western Frontier, in: The Quilt Digest, No. 1, San Francisco, 1983, pp. 6-13.

126. Robert Cargo, Long Remembered—An Alabama Pioneer and Her Quilts, in: The Quilt Digest 3, 1985, pp. 63-65.

127. Barbara Brackman, Chronological Index to Pieced Quilt Patterns 1775-1825, in: Uncoverings, Vol. 4, 1983, pp. 104-110.

128. Carrie Hall and Rose Kretsinger, Romance of the Patchwork Quilt in America, Kansas, 1935, pp. 56-57, No. 12.

129. Robert Bishop, Quilts, Coverlets, Rugs and Samplers, New York, 1982, p. 112.

130. Barbara Brackman, Chronological Index..., pp. 99ff.

131. Hall & Kretsinger, pp. 56-57, No. 13, and pp. 54-55, No. 9.

132. Judy Mathieson, Some Published Sources of Design Inspiration for the Quilt Pattern Mariner's Compass—17th to 20th Century, in: Uncoverings, Vol. 2, 1981, pp. 11-18.

133. Carter Houck & Myron Miller, American Quilts and How to Make Them, New York, 1975, p. 159.

134. My descriptions are based essentially on Linda Lipsett, A Piece of Ellen's Dress, in: The Quilt Digest, 2, San Francisco, 1984, and Remember me—Women and Their Friendship Quilts, San Francisco, 1985.

135. Basic literature: Dena S. Katzenberg, Baltimore Album Quilts, Baltimore Museum of Art, 1982; Carleton Safford and Robert Bishop, American Quilts and Coverlets, New York, 1972, pp. 145ff.

136. Patricia T. Herr, The Pennsylvania Germans—A Celebration of Their Arts 1683-850, Philadelphia Museum of Art.

137. Dena S. Katzenberg, op. cit., p. 14.

138. Penny McMorris, Crazy Quilts, New York, 1984, p. 11.

139. Ruth Finley, Old Patchwork Quilts and the Women Who Made Them, 1929, reprinted 1983, Charles T. Branford Co., p. 32.

140. Virginia Gunn, Victorian Silk Template Patchwork in American Periodicals 1850-1875, in: Uncoverings, Vol. 4, 1983, pp. 9-25.

141. Blocks are not normally sewn in England. Instead, individual parts (for example, diamonds or hexagons) are tacked to paper patterns and sewn together in succession. Only when the piece of work is finished are the patterns removed.

142. Penny McMorris, op. cit., p. 12.

143. Virginia Gunn, Crazy Quilts and Outline Quilts 1876-1893, in: Uncoverings, Vol. 5, 1984, pp. 131-152.

144. Virginia Gunn, Crazy Quilts, op. cit., p. 132.

145. Penny McMorris, op. cit., pp. 63ff.

146. My descriptions are based mainly on Penny McMorris and Virginia Gunn, as well as Sally Garoutte, The Development of Crazy Quilts, in: Quilter's Journal, Fall 1978, pp. 13-18.

147. Rachel and Kenneth Pellman, The World of Amish Quilts, Intercourse, Pennsylvania, 1984, pp. 8-9. The Amish believe that their way of life and their actions in every phase of their lives must reflect their firm faith. Being in this world without being of this world is a concept that they consequently practice (R. & K. Pellmann, p. 104). Through their own strict type of clothing, their own language (German) and their independent school system, they separate themselves outwardly from sciety in general, which they call "the English" and whose society they call "of the world". The religious and friendly community into which they are born, and for which they must decide as young adults, becomes a conscience for each of them. On the basis of the "order" they have set up, the community decides whether its membership is righteous and what they shall do and allow. The Amish rely on the support and friendship of the family, community and church. It is the haven that protects them from the destructive influence of the world. Integration into the "English" community results in exclusion from the sect. Everything that could have given impetus to the alienation is banned. For this reason the Amish take a very skeptical attitude to the achievements of modern industry. They refuse to use electricity, because the constant availability of electric power could disturb the unity of the family. Instead they live with gas lamps that must be filled, lit and carried from room to room. This decision in and of itself provides for the physical togetherness of the family every evening. They use diesel engines to generate the energy they need to cool the milk on their farms, and to operate household apliances and tools whose use does not go against the community's principles. Horses and mules are used in place of autos and tractors that could tempt them into making trips that would take them away from everyday family life.

148. Robert Bishop and Elizabeth Safanda, A Gallery of Amish Quilts, New York, 1976, p. 7.

149. Bishop & Safanda, p. 25.

150. R. & K. Pellman, p. 102.

151. Bishop & Safanda, p. 11; Frances Lichten, Folk Art of Rural Pennsylvania, 1946.

152. Bishop & Safanda, p. 16.

153. Phyllis Haders, Sunshine and Shadow—The Amish and Their Quilts, New York, 1976.

154. Bishop & Safanda, p. 23.

155. Jonathan Holstein, The Pieced Quilt—An American Design Tradition, Boston, 1973, p. 99.

156. Bishop & Safanda, p. 25.

157. R. & K. Pellman, pp. 68ff.

158. Cuesta Benberry, Afro-American Quilts, in: Quilting II with Penny McMorris, Bowling Green, Ohio, 1982, p. 53. Basic literature on this theme: Maude Wahlman, The Art of Afro-American Quiltmaking: Origin, Development and Significance, Indiana University Press, 1982; Maude Wahlman and John Scully, Afro-American Folk Arts and Crafts, New York, 1982.

159. Cuesta Benberry, Afro-American Women and Quilts, in: Uncoverings, Vol. 1, 1980, pp. 64-67.

160. Cuesta Benberry, Quilting II, p. 53.

161. Lacy Folmer Bullard, Once Out Of Time, Charleston Museum, North Carolina, in: Quilt Digest 3, San Francisco, 1985.

162. Gladys Mary Fry about Harriet Powers, in: Quilting II, pp. 54-55.

163. Maude Wahlman, Design Characteristics, in: Quilting II, p. 55. 164. Beverly Rush and Lassie Wittmann, Seminole Patchwork, Seattle, 1982, pp. 1, 97ff and 111 ff.

165. Maude Wahlman, Design Characteristics, in: Quilting II, p. 56.

166. Cuesta Benberry, White Perceptions of Blacks in Quilts and Related Media, in: Uncoverings, Vol. 4, 1983, pp. 59ff.

167. Elizabeth Akana, Ku'u Hae Aloha, in: Quilt Digest 2, San Francisco, 1984, p. 70. Basic literature on this theme: Elizabeth Akana, Hawaiian Quilting: A Fine Art, with the exhibition catalog of the Mission House Museum, Honolulu, 1981; Thomas K. Woodard and Blanche Greenstein, Hawaiian Quilts: Treasures of an Island Folk Art, exhibition catalog of the American Museum of Folk Art, New York, 1979.

168. E. Akana, op. cit., p. 72.

169. Kynn Synder Rice, The Hawaiian Quilt, in: Art & Antiques, May-June 1981, p. 102.

170. Carleton Safford and Robert Bishop, America's Quilts and Coverlets, New York, 1980, p. 198.

171. Joyce Cross, Hawaiian Applique, in: Quilting II with Penny McMorris, Bowling Green, Ohio, 1982, p. 45.

172. E. Akana, op. cit., p. 72.

173. Joyce Gross, op. cit., p. 47.

174. E. Akana, op. cit., pp. 74-76.

175. Barbara Brackman, Dating Old Quilts, Part 3, in: Quilter's Newsletter Magazine, November-December 1984, p. 16.

176. Barbara Brackman, op. cit., p. 17.

177. Barbara Brackman, Quilts from Feed Sacks, in: Quilter's Newsletter Magazine, October 1985, p. 38.

178. Barbara Brackman, Quilts from Feed Sacks, pp. 36ff.

179. Jinny Beyer, The Quilter's Album of Blocks and Borders, London, 1980, p. 131.

180. Jinny Beyer, op. cit., p. 136.

181. Robert Bishop, Quilts, Coverlets, Rugs & Samplers, New York, 1982, p. 105.

182. Jinny Beyer, op. cit., p. 135.

183. Robert Bishop, op. cit., p. 150.

184. Robert Bishop in: American Folk Art, New York, 1983, catalog for an exhibition of the American folk Art Museum, New York, in the City Museum, Munich, and the Altona Museum, Hamburg, p. 6.

185. Particular geographic and economic conditions in the Southern Appalachian area led to an unbroken practice of traditional quilting from colonial times to this day. Barbara von Roemer, Patchwork and Quilts in the USA, in: Deutsches Textilforum 2/84, p. 27.

186. Barbara von Roemer, op. cit., pp. 26-28.

187. English Quilter's Guild, 2000 (1983) members since 1979; Netherlands Quilter's Guild, 500 (1985) members since 1983; German Patchwork Guild, 800 (1988) members since 1985.

188. Barbara von Roemer, op. cit., p. 27.
189. Catalog: The Artist and The Quilt, Ed. Charlotte Robinson, New York, 1983.
190. Catalog: The Artist's Quilts, Ed. Lucy Strauss, La Jolla Museum, California, 1981.
191. Catalog: The Quilt—New Directions for an American Tradition, Quilt National, Schiffer Publ. Ltd., Exton, Pennsylvania, 1983; Catalog: Quilts— The State of an Art, Quilt National, Schiffer Publ. Ltd., Exton, Pennsylvania, 1985.
192. Michael James, The State of an Art, in the 1983 Quilt National Catalog, p. 6.
193. Helpful hints are found in: Robert Bishop, Quilts, Coverlets, Rugs & Samplers, The Knopf Collector's Guide to American Antiques, New York, 1982; Phyllis Haders, The Main Street Pocket Guide to Quilts, Pittstown, new Jersey, 1982.
194. Patsy Orlofsky, The Collector's Guide for the Care of Quilts in the Home, Quilt Digest 2, San Francisco, 1984—definitely the only advice in this area to be taken seriously. Advice for mounting of quilts can be obtained from The Smithsonian Institution, The National Museum of History and Technology, Washington D.C. 20560, (Mounting Large Textiles on a Frame, Division of Textiles)

Bibliography

There is an almost incalculable quantity of English-language publications on the subject of patchwork and quilts. Instruction books, which one can even buy in the supermarket in the USA, have been excluded as long as they do not include any important aspects of quilt research. Above all, books are listed here that make possible further study and immersion in the subject. I could only touch briefly on much that is said there. The footnotes hint at more definite data that the bibliography cannot cover. Only there are more specialized matters referred to.

My work offers an overview of the status of research as of the middle of 1985, on the basis of the following publications:

Akana, Elizabeth, Hawaiian Quilting, A Fine Art; Catalog of the Mission House Museum, Honolulu, 1981.

American Folk Art, American Folk Art Museum, Catalog of Exhibitions in the City Museum, Munich, and the Altona Museum, Hamburg, 1982-83.

Bacon, Lenice Ingram, American Patchwork Quilts, William Morrow & Co., New York, 1973.

Bannister, Barbara, The United States Patchwork Book, Dover Publ., New York, 1976.

Betterton, Sheila, Quilts and Coverlets from the American Museum in Britain, Butler & Tanner Ltd., London-Bath, 1978.

Beyer, Jinny, The Quilter's Album of Blocks and Borders, Bell & Hyman Ltd., London, 1980.

Beyer, Jinny, Patchwork Patterns, EPM Publications, McLean VA, 1979.

Bishop, Robert, New Discoveries in American Quilts, E. P. Dutton, New York, 1975.

Bishop, Robert, and Safanda, Elizabeth, A Gallery of Amish Quilts, Design Diversity from a Plain People, E. P. Dutton, New York, 1976.

Bishop, Robert, et al., Quilts, Coverlets, Rugs and Samplers, The Knopf Collector's Guide, New York, 1982.

Bridgeman, Harriet, and Drury, Elizabeth, Geschichte der Textilkunst, Ravensburg, 1978.

Christopherson, Katy, The Political and Campaign Quilt, Lexington KY, 1984.

Clabburn, Pamela, Patchwork, Shire Album 101, Aylesbury GB, 1983.

Clark, Hazel, Textile Printing, Shire Album 135, Aylesbury GB, 1985.

Colby, Averil, Patchwork, B. T. Batsford Ltd., London, 1958, reprinted 1976 and 1983.

Colby, Averil, Quilting, B. T. Batsford Ltd., London, 1972, reprinted 1976 and 1983.

Deutsches Textilforum Heft Juni 1984, Patchwork und Quilt, Hannover, 1984.

Finley, Ruth, Old Patchwork Quilts and the Women Who Made Them, Philadelphia, 1929; Charles T. Branford, Newton Center MA, 1971, reprinted 1983.

Freeman, June, Quilting, Patchwork and Applique/ 1700-1982—Sewing as a Woman's Art, Crafts Council, London, 1983.

Geijer, Agnes, A History of Textile Art, Pasold Research Fund, Stockholm, 1979.

Haders, Phyllis, Sunshine and Shadow—The Amish and Their Quilts, Universe books, New York, 1976.

Haders, Phyllis, The Main Street Pocket Guide to Quilts, The Main Street Press, Pittstown NJ, 1983.

Hall, Carrie A. and Kretsinger, Rose G., The Romance of the Patchwork Quilt in America, Bonanza Books, n.d., reprint of the 1935 edition.

Hechtlinger, Adelaide, American Quilts, Quilting and Patchwork, Galahad Books, New York, 1974.

Herr, Patricia T., The Pennsylvania Germans—Celebration of Their Arts 1683-1850, Philadelphia Museum of Art.

Holstein, Jonathan, The Pieced Quilt—An American Design Tradition, New York Graphic Society, Boston, 1973.

Holstein, Jonathan, and Finley, John, Kentucky Quilts 1800-1900, The Kentucky Quilt Project, Pantheon Books, New York, 1982.

Homage to America—Two Hundred Years of American Quilts, Collection of Edwin Binney and Gail Binney-Winslow, R. K. Press, San Francisco, 1984.

Houck, Carter, and Miller, Myron, American Quilts and How to Make Them, Charles Scribner's Sons, New York, 1975.

Ickis, Marguerite, Quilt Making and Collecting, New York, 1949, reprinted.

Irish Patchwork, Ed. Alex Meldrum, Kilkenny Design Workshops, 1979.

Irwin, John Rice, A People and Their Quilts, Schiffer Publ., Exton PA, 1983.

Katzenberg, Dena S., Baltimore Album Quilts, Baltimore Museum of Art, Exhibition Catalog, 1982.

Khin, Yvonne, The Collector's Dictionary of Quilt Names and Patterns, Acropolis Books, Washington D.C., 1980.

Klüser, Verena, Amerikanische Quilts, Schellmann & Klüser, Munich, 1983.

Lichten, Frances, Folk Art of Rural Pennsylvania, Charles Scribner's Sons, New York, 1946.

Mattera, Joanne, The Quiltmaker's Art—Contemporary Quilts and Their Makers, Lark Books, Asheville NC, 1982.

Mattern-Pabel, Patchwork Quilt, Verlag M&H Schaper, Hannover, 1981.

McKim, Ruby, One Hundred and One Patchwork Patterns, Dover Publ., New York, 1962.

McMorris, Penny, Crazy Quilts, E. P. Dutton, New York, 1984.

McMorris, Penny, Quilting II, Bowling Green State University, WBGU-TV Instruction Book, Ohio, 182.

Montgomery, Florence, Printed Textiles: English and American Cottons and Linens 1700-1850, Viking Press, New York, 1970.

Morgan, Mary, and Mosteller, Dee, Trapunto, Charles Scribner's Sons, New York, 1977.

Nelson, Cyril, and Houck, Carter, The Quilt Engagement Calendar Treasury, E. P. Dutton, New York, 1982.

Orlofsky, Patsy & Myron, Quilts in America, McGraw Hill, New York, 1974.

Otto Lipsett, Linda, Remember Me—Women and Their Friendship Quilts, The Quilt Digest Press, San Francisco, 1985.

Pellman, Rachel and Kenneth, The World of Amish Quilts, Good Books, Intercourse PA, 1984.

Pettit, Florence, America's Printed and Painted Fabrics 1600-1900, Hasting's House, New York, 1970.

Pottinger, David, Quilts from the Indiana Amish—A Regional Collection, E. P. Dutton, New York, 1983.

Quilt Digest, Volumes 1, 2, 3, 4, The Quilt Digest Press, San Francisco, 1983, 1984, 1985, 1986.

The Quilt—New Directions for an American Tradition, Quilt National Catalog, Athens OH, 1983.

Quilts—The State of an Art, Quilt National Catalog, Athens OH, 1985.

Reichelt-Jordan, Margit, Patchwork und Applikationen, Heyne, Munich, 1982.

Robinson, Charlotte, Ed., The Artist and the Quilt—Catalog, Alfred A. Knopf, New York, 1983.

Roemer, Barbara von, Patchwork und Quilts, Paul Haupt Verlag, Stuttgart-Bern, 1982.

Rush, Beverly, and Wittmann, Lassie, Seminole Patchwork, Madrona Publ., Seattle, 1982.

Safford, Charleton L., and Bishop, Robert, America's Quilts and Coverlets, E. P. Dutton, New York, 1982.

Schaepper, Linda, Exhibition Catalog, Paris, 1982.

Strauss, Ludy, The Artist's Quilts-Catalog, La Jolla Museum, California, 1981.

Stevens, Napua, The Hawaiian Quilt, Service Printers, Honolulu, 1971.

Uncoverings, Vol. 1-6, Ed. Sally Garroutte, American Quilt Study Group, Mill Valley CA, 1980, 1981, 1982, 1983, 1984, 1985.

Victoria and Albert Museum, Notes on Patchwork, Her Majesty's Stationery Office, London, 1949.

Wiss, Audrey, and Douglas, Folk Quilts and how to Recreate Them, The Main Street Press, Pittstown NJ, 1983.

Woodard, Thomas K., and Greenstein, Blanche, Hawaiian Quilts: Treasures of an Island Folk Art, Catalog of the American Folk Museum, New York, 1979.

Woodard, Thomas K., and Greenstein, Blanche, The Poster Book of Quilts, E. P. Dutton, New York, 1984.

Textile Handicrafts in Asia, Africs, Europe and South America.

African Art, Periodical of the University of California at Los Angeles.

Bussabarger, R. I., and Robins, Dashew B., The Everyday Art of India, New York, 1968.

Casal, Jose/, The People and Art of the Philippines, University of California Press, Museum of Cultural History, Los Angeles, 1981.

Elson, Vickie C., Dowries from Kutch: A Women's Folk Art Tradition in India, University of California Press, Museum of Cultural History, Los Angeles, 1975.

Faigre, Thorvald, Tents, Architecture of the Nomads, London, 1979.

Fischer, Eberhard, Rural Craftsmen and Their Work, National Institute of Design, Ahmedabad, 1970.

Fischer, Eberhard, and Haku Shah, Kunsttraditionen in Nordindien, Catalog of the special exhibition "Unbekanntes Indien", Rietberg Museum im Helmhaus, Zürich, 1972.

Gardi, Rene/e, Unter Afrikanischen Handwerkern, Bern, 1969.

Geijer, Agnes, Oriental Textiles in Sweden, Copenhagen, 1951.

Gittinger, Mattiebelle, Splendid Symbols—Textiles and Traditionsin Indonesia, Washington, 1979.

Gold der Skythen aus der Eremitage Leningrad, Catalog of the State Antique Collection, Munich, 1984.

Haake, Annegret, Javanische Batik, Verlag M&H Schaper, Hannover, 1980.

Hall, M., Indisches Kunsthandwerk, Berlin, 1971.

Hartmann, Günther, Molakana—Volkskunst der Cuna, Panama, Publication of the Völkerkunde Museum, Berlin, 1980.

Hunt Kahlenberg, Mary, Textile Traditions in Indonesia, University of California Press, Museum of Cultural History, Los Angeles, 1977.

Irwin, John, and Hall, M., Indian Painted and Printed Fabrics: Indian Embroideries, Vol. 1 and 2 of The Historic Textiles of India at the Calico Museum of Ahmedabad, 1971-1973.

Jaques, R., Deutsche Textilkunst, 1953.

Kaplan, N., and Ivanov, S., Ed., In the Land of Reindeer, Leningrad, 1974.

Lamb, Alastair and Venice, The Lamb collection of West African Narrow Strip Weaving, Textile Museum, Washington D.C., 1975.

Lamb, Venice, West African Weaving, London, 1980.

Lewis, Paul and Elaine, Völker im Goldenen Dreieck, Edition Hansjörg Meyer, Stuttgart, 1984.

Mack, John and Picton, John, African Textiles, British Museum of Mankind, London, 1979.

McCabe, Elliot, Inger, Tambal—Patchwork—Batik, New York, 1984.

Menzel, Brigitte, Textilien aus Westafrika, 3 Vol., Museum für Völkerkunde, Berlin, 1972.

Meyer-Heisig, Erich, Weberei, Nadelwerk, Zeugdruck, Munich, 1956.

Meyerowitz, Eva L., The Akan of Ghana, London, 1958. Mohanty, Bijoi Chandra, Study of Contemporary Textile Crafts of India: Applique/ Craft of Orissa, Ahmedabad, 1980.

Noma, Seiroku, Japanese Costume and Textile Arts, Weatherhill-Heibonsha, Tokyo, 1974.

Price, Sally and Richard, Afro-American Arts of the Surinam Rain Forest, University of California Press, Museum of Cultural History, Los Angeles, 1980.

Sieber, Roy, African Textiles and Decorative Arts, Museum of Modern Art, New York, 1972.

Textiles of Africa, Ed. Idens, Dale & Ponting, K. G. Bath, 1980.

Textiles of Japan III: Okinawan, Ainu and Foreign Designs, Japan Textile Colour Center, London, 1980.

Türkische Kunst und Kultur in Osmanischer Zeit, Exhibition Catalog, Vol. 1 & 2, Bongers, Recklinghausen, 1980.

Tyrell, Tribal Peoples of Southern Africa, Books of Africa, Capetown, 1968.

Wahlman, Maude, The Art of Afro-American Quiltmaking: Origin, Development and Significance, Indiana University Press, Bloomington, 1982.

Wahlman, Maude, and Scully, John, Afro-American Folk Arts and Crafts, New York, 1982.

Westphal-Hallbusch, Sigrid, and Soltkahn, Gisela, Mützen aus Zentralasien und Persien, Museum für Völkerkunde, Berlin, 1976.

Translator's Note

It is only fair to mention the book to which I referred when translating this book into English:
MacDonald, Jessie, and Shafer, Marian H., *Let's Make A Patchwork Quilt*, Farm Journal, Philadelphia, 1980,
and to thank my wife for making it available to me and for pointing out the difference between the Aster and Dresden Plate patterns.

Photo Index

Nimwegen, Nijmeegs Museum Commanderie von Sint Jan: 36.
Nottingham, Pauline Burbidge (Photo by John Coles): 113.
Nottingham, Museum of Costumes and Textiles: 88.
Nuremberg, Germanisches Nationalmuseum: 43.
Nuremberg, Kunsthaus Klinger: 92.
Oslo, Ethografisk Museum (Photo by Elisabeth Sletten): 27.
Paris, Service photographique de la Re/union des muse/es nationaux: 1.
Recklinghausen, Verlag Aurel Bongers, from Türkische Kunst II: 12.
Rom, Biblioteca Vaticana: 14.
Schlitz, Hans Deibel: 41.
Somerset Village (Massachusetts), Michael James: 109.
Stockholm, Antivarisk-Topografiska Arkivet (Photo by G. Hildebrand): 33.
Stockton (California), The Haggin Museum: 93.
Stuttgart, Auktionshaus Dr. Fritz Nagel: 19.
Washington, Smithsonian Institution: 54.
Winterthur (Delaware), Henry Francis Du Pont Winterthur Museum: 55.
Williamsburg, Abby Aldrich Rockefeller Folk Art Center: 57.